101 More Dance
Games for Children

Other Smart Fun Books

101 Music Games for Children by Jerry Storms

101 More Music Games for Children by Jerry Storms

101 Drama Games for Children by Paul Rooyackers

101 More Drama Games for Children by Paul Rooyackers

101 Dance Games for Children by Paul Rooyackers

101 Movement Games for Children by Huberta Wiertsema

101 Language Games for Children by Paul Rooyackers

Coming Soon:

Yoga Games for Children by Danielle Bersma and Marjoke Visscher

Ordering

Trade bookstores in the U.S. and Canada, please contact:

Publishers Group West
1700 Fourth Street, Berkeley CA 94710
Phone: (800) 788-3123   Fax: (510) 528-3444

Hunter House books are available at bulk discounts for course adoptions;
to qualifying community, health-care, and government organizations;
and for special promotions and fund-raising. For details please contact:

Special Sales Department
Hunter House Inc., PO Box 2914, Alameda CA 94501-0914
Phone: (510) 865-5282   Fax: (510) 865-4295
E-mail: ordering@hunterhouse.com

Individuals can order our books from most bookstores,
by calling **(800) 266-5592**, or from our
website at **www.hunterhouse.com**

1<u>0</u>1 MORE

Dance Games

FOR

Children

New Fun and Creativity with Movement

Paul Rooyackers

Translated by Amina Marix Evans
with Photographs by Rob Webster

a Hunter House *Smart Fun* book

First published in the Netherlands in 1994 by Panta Rhei as
100 Nieuwe Dansspelen

Library of Congress Cataloging-in-Publication Data
Rooyackers, Paul.
　　　[Honderd nieuwe dansspelen. English]
　　　101 more dance games for children : new fun and creativity with movement / Paul Rooyackers ; translated by Amina Marix Evans.
　　　　　　　p. cm. — (A Hunter House SmartFun book)
　　　Includes index.
　　　ISBN 0-89793-384-2 (spiral) — ISBN 0-89793-383-4 (pbk.)
　　　1. Games. 2. Dance for children. I. Title: One hundred one more dance games for children. II. Title: One hundred and one more dance games for children. III. Title. IV. Series.
GV1203 .R5913 2002
790.1'922—dc21　　　　　　　　　　　　　　　　　　　　　　2002075932

Project Credits

Cover Design and Book Production:
　Jil Weil

Book Design: Hunter House

Developmental and Copy Editor:
　Ashley Chase

Proofreader: John David Marion

Acquisitions Editor: Jeanne Brondino

Editor: Alexandra Mummery

Editorial Assistant: Caroline Knapp

Editorial and Production Intern:
　Claire Reilly-Shapiro

Publicity Coordinator:
　Earlita K. Chenault

Sales & Marketing Coordinator:
　Jo Anne Retzlaff

Customer Service Manager:
　Christina Sverdrup

Order Fulfillment: Lakdhon Lama

Administrator: Theresa Nelson

Computer Support: Peter Eichelberger

Publisher: Kiran S. Rana

Printed and Bound by Bang Printing, Brainerd, Minnesota

Manufactured in the United States of America
9 8 7 6 5 4 3 2 1　　　First Edition　　　03 04 05 06 07

Contents

*A detailed list of the games indicating
appropriate age groups begins on the next page.*

List of Games

List of Games, continued

List of Games, continued

List of Games, continued

List of Games, continued

Dance Projects from Around the World

Preface

This book contains one hundred and one new dance games. It is both a sequel to and a further development of the original book, *101 Dance Games for Children*. Like the original, this book includes many exercises to develop basic dance skills, such as warm-ups, story dances, dances with props, and introduction dances. However, this book builds on the first book with new types of games and even more opportunities to explore. For example, players discover unusual, whole-body movements in the body dances. The open-air dances give them the chance to explore the outside world as a stage. Players explore world dance in the final section, a series of projects inspired by the dance traditions of different cultures. Many of the games will result in works ready for performance at a parents' night or other event. In this book you will also find a greater number of games that are specifically designed for teenagers in junior high and high school. Together, the two books offer a wealth of possibilities for planning play sessions.

These games are ideally suited for dance classes in a school, camp, or workshop setting. They are also useful for physical education, drama, and music classes. They can be used as activities for summer-camp and after-school groups. Many of the games could be adapted for use in creative therapy.

This book is designed in particular for those who love to dance and wish to get down to work on fun, practical ideas without needing formal training in dance. The games have been created and developed in a classroom situation. They are described in detail so that you can lead them without a great deal of experience in dance or game direction. Still, practice the activities yourself before using them with a group.

101 More Dance Games would never have come about without a host of ideas from the dancers young and old whom I have taught in the last decades. This book is dedicated to all of them.

Have fun!

Paul Rooyackers
The Netherlands, 2001

For easy reading, we have alternated use of the male and female pronouns. Of course, every "he" also means "she," and vice versa!

Introduction

Objectives of the Dance Games

The dance games serve various educational goals applicable to dance, physical education, drama, and music classes. They are also valuable to players' personal and social development. The games are designed to

- **foster creativity**
  None of these dance games involve memorizing standard steps. The games challenge players to improvise and experiment with unusual movements. Players explore the world around them and come up with creative ways to express emotions and ideas through movement. The dance games also provide dozens of opportunities for players to create and develop their own choreography.

- **improve physical conditioning**
  The games are excellent exercise. While dancing, players develop their strength, balance, agility, flexibility, and reaction time. They become more aware of their bodies and how they move.

- **build social skills: cooperation, trust, respect**
  The games in this book give players ample opportunities to work in pairs, small groups, and as a class. Players collaborate on performance pieces: Together they improvise; create dance steps; make decisions about staging, casting, and so on; and perform in front of an audience. Dancing together, the group builds mutual trust and respect.

- **build self-confidence**
  The dance games let players perform in a noncompetitive

setting where there are no stars: Everyone has a chance to shine. Practicing self-expression in a fun, low-pressure context helps players overcome shyness and stage fright.

Information for the Leader

The Leader's Role

The leader plays many important roles in conducting these dance games: muse, stage manager, ringmaster, cheerleader, and more. Here are a few tips for leading the games. *101 Dance Games* provides even more suggestions. As leader, be sure to do the following:

- **Dance.** Giving a dance class without dancing yourself is almost unthinkable, and not possible from a practical point of view. Do not teach a dance exercise if you don't know what you are talking about or if you don't want to dance yourself. If you are going to teach others to dance, you yourself must feel it. That is rule number one.

  Always begin dancing right away—dancing is something you have to do, not talk about too much.

- **Choose games you enjoy and believe in.** Don't teach a dance game if you don't understand it or if you didn't find it interesting when you tried it for yourself.

- **Always prepare the dance games in advance, preferably with other people.** If you are teaching with a partner or aide, practice and try out games with each other before you play them with a group. This way you will be alerted to the points where things can go wrong. You will also see where you can correct each other and support each other during the game. Join in when others lead the game—this will stimulate the children. Good preparation is half the work! Be prepared to stray from your plan, though. Watch the group carefully and stop or change the game if it is not going well.

- **Create a good atmosphere before, during, and after dancing.** Bring the group into *your* atmosphere; that is one of the most important things a leader needs to accomplish. A leader with a bad attitude will simply see that attitude reflected back. Make sure the room is suitable for dancing, with plenty of space, light, and air. Always open a window before you begin so that no one will develop headaches or dizziness. *101 Dance Games* gives more advice about preparing the room for dancing.

- **Anticipate and prepare for any mishaps.** Make sure players warm up properly to prevent muscle-pulls. When large numbers of players dance around carelessly, collisions are likely. With a little foresight, you should be able to avoid accidents. Agree on an emergency signal that means players should freeze—this way you can stop a potential collision in time.

- **Learn about the players before you start a dance game.** If you are working with an unfamiliar group, always find out as much as you can about the group members. Make sure that you know how much dance experience the group has and whether any players have physical problems. Advance information about a group can often prevent problems from occurring.

- **Agree on signals for directing play.** You may need to give a signal to begin a game or perhaps to interrupt the game if something goes wrong. At a group's first meeting, demonstrate a few simple signals to the group and explain what they mean. You might create signals for starting and stopping play, for freezing the action in case of emergency, for winding a game up, or for increasing concentration.

I saw a good example of signals while observing a class. One half of the group was watching the others presenting a dance piece. The leader called out a few words that were effective and clearly familiar to the participants:

1. "Dancers ready?"

2. "Audience ready?"

3. "House lights down!"

4. "Spotlight on!"

At the second signal, the audience members knew they should be quiet and that the show would soon begin. At the fourth signal, the performers started dancing immediately, fully prepared. This system worked extremely well, and you can easily develop something similar of your own. The important thing is that the group recognizes the ritual.

- **Think about how to guide players through the games.** Some games involve guided improvisations, while others give players free reign. Make it quite clear when players should take the initiative and when they should follow your guidelines. Explain the concept of the game briefly, and get players dancing. You can bring in more ideas and variations as the game goes on—we call this side-coaching. You coach the group through any problems, give players inspiration in the form of action words, or change the tempo, force, or level of the dance. (See the section on dance terms below.) Practice an effective voice for leading the games. You must be audible, but a loud, grating voice might ruin the atmosphere you are trying to create.

- **Teach the players to listen to you and to each other.** Listening and allowing others to finish what they are saying aids not only the progress of the game but the enjoyment as well. Never begin a game until it is quiet and you have sufficient concentration to explain the game properly. Players should not make remarks when someone else is dancing, nor should they walk away or otherwise disturb the action. You should be very firm about this because concentration is essential to expressive and fluid dancing.

- **Allow criticism—but only constructive criticism.** Teach players how to ask questions about other players' performances. Limiting players to questions rather than comments should help keep the discussion positive. Intervene immediately if you see that someone is planning to make a negative comment.

- **Finish each dance game with a silence or some other clear conclusion.** You might choose to follow a game with a discussion, inviting input from all the players.

Dance Terms

Movement is always tricky to capture in words. A few terms useful in explaining and leading the dance games are discussed below.

Action Words

Action words are simply verbs describing action. You can use vivid verbs to inspire players to explore new ways of moving. Effective action words include *jump, fall, dangle, flop, roll, turn, float, bend, saunter, drag, drift, slink, wobble, swing, shuffle, vibrate, pull, glide, bounce,* and *push.* Try to avoid bland words such as *walk* or *run,* because they will not provide any creative stimulus.

Tempo

Tempo refers to the speed of the movement: Is it fast or slow? Help players add variety to their dances by asking them to change the tempo of their dancing. The same movement can seem very different depending on whether it is done slowly and languidly or swiftly and abruptly.

Power or Force

When we discuss the power or force of a dance, we are talking about a spectrum ranging from strong, heavy, and intense movements at one extreme to light and floating movements at the other. Help players see how varying the force of a dance can make the climax come across even more powerfully.

Height Levels/Use of Space

Another area in which players can add variety and interest to their dances is height levels. Players can dance while crouching down, or rolling on the ground, or stretching up with arms raised and toes pointed. Encourage players to change the levels of their dances often. They can also vary their use of space by exploring every corner of the dance area and by making both large and small movements.

Movement Shapes

In addition to using action words, you can inspire players by calling out adjectives describing movement shapes. For example, you might ask players to make their bodies rounded or angular, jagged, wispy, or long and lean. Players should make their poses, their movements, and the path they trace through the space match the shapes you describe.

Emotions

Last but not least, encourage players to use their bodies to express different emotions as they dance. Ask them to create dances showing disappointment, anger, pain, pride, dejection, fear, love, happiness, exuberance, and so on.

Instant Choreography

You can combine the dance elements above (action words, tempo, power, height, shape, and emotion) to create instant choreography. Players will be able to put together and perform a dance on the spot.

You might start with the action words *bounce, wobble,* and *roll.* Add the following dance elements: a quick tempo, high power, constantly changing height levels, rounded shapes, and a merry feeling. Form groups of four or more who choose a different sequence of action words and start from different positions in the room (or on the stage), and a dance about superballs has begun....

Take a few action words, some dance elements, and a piece of music. Put them together in your head and work the details out with the group: instant choreography!

How to Combine Games to Form a Comprehensive Program

Each of the dance games can stand alone. The dance games may also be used as the core of a dance program. In the latter case, you can give each class session a logical structure by choosing games to serve various functions. The games are grouped according to type, and each section begins with a brief introduction about the type of game covered. Different types of games can be combined for a play session.

The following types of game are included:

- introduction dances
- body dances
- object dances
- story dances
- animal dances
- character dances
- open-air dances

- painting dances

- dance maps

- musical dances

- dance projects from around the world

The phases of a dance session are described below. We also follow an example dance session through the various phases. Note that some of the longer games are designed to make up entire dance sessions and have been organized into phases already. See game 48 (Skating), game 49 (Spring Dance), and game 53 (Party Dance).

Planning Phase

Before leading a dance session you need to know what you are trying to achieve. What do you want to teach the students? What should they explore? What do you want them to discover?

Choose a very general main objective for the session, such as "learning cooperation." You might extend a main objective over the course of several sessions. Then describe your more specific secondary objective: What exactly do you want to teach the group in this session? For example, you might decide to have partners work on balancing together in order to teach them how to cooperate in dance. Once you have worked out your objectives, decide on action words and movement shapes for the session. (See the section on dance terms above.)

Example: For a dance session for high school students, you might choose the following objectives:

Main objective: learning to dance with objects

Secondary objective: trying out fluid movements using a single object, to flowing music

Action words: lift, push, pull, float

Movement shapes: supple, fluid

Phase One: Introduction/Warm-Up

The session should always start with a warm-up: a short game to create the right atmosphere. The players will likely enter the room with their minds on other concerns; they need to work loose from distractions to concentrate fully on the dance games. You will need to bring the group into the right frame of mind. This can be done using introduction dances (see page 13), body dances (see page 27), or story dances (see page 73). This phase also introduces the concepts that will be covered in the dance session.

Example: You might introduce the dance session on objects by displaying photos of dancers performing with objects. Discuss how the dancers in the photos are using the objects and how the objects seem to be influencing their dance moves. Now make marks on the floor with chalk or tape to represent some invisible objects. When the players dance, they must not cross into these areas.

Phase Two: Exploration
In the exploration phase, players experiment freely with the activity you have chosen. They might explore unusual movements, as in the body dances (see page 27), or they might experiment with all the different possibilities that come along with using a particular setting or prop. The emphasis of this phase is on experimentation, rather than performance.

Example: Game 40 (Dancing with Objects) would be ideal for the exploration phase of the dance session on objects. Players dance around the objects for a while, without touching them. From the sidelines, suggest that players let the objects' shapes influence their dance movements. Ask them to vary the level, tempo, and force of their dance moves.

Phase Three: Improvisation
In the improvisation phase of the session, players put together the movements and ideas they experimented with in the exploration phase. They improvise a dance alone or in small groups.

Example: You could use game 41 (A Broom Is Your Dance Partner) for the improvisation phase of our example dance session on objects. Players focus on one object and build an improvised dance around it, trying out a series of fluid movements to music.

Phase Four: Presentation
A presentation at the end of a session can last a few minutes or much longer with more experienced dancers. With beginners, it is better to keep it short—even 30 seconds can be long enough. Choose music fragments of that length so that at first the presentations are over

quickly and the participants will look forward to doing more next time.

Example: Players work in pairs to perform a dance piece using objects.

Phase Five: Cool-Down and Discussion
A moment of calm should follow the performance phase. Games emphasizing concentration or relaxation, such as game 7 (Sleep Tight) or game 83 (Art Gallery), should work well for this phase.

The players leave a session with a wealth of impressions and experiences. They may well be excited by what happened, or perhaps something touched them deeply. It is very important that you discuss the exercises and performances carefully with players. Be constructive and inspiring in your criticism. Comment on positive aspects that the players can build on personally and as a group. Players need to feel they are in a process of development that you are carefully guiding.

You might want to leave a notebook in the room where players can write down questions or comments. That way players can give you feedback even if time does not allow for a group discussion, or if they have comments they feel uncomfortable making in front of the others.

Example: You could round off the dance session on objects with a discussion of how objects can be used in a dance and how using different objects affects the movements and mood of a dance.

Key to the Icons Used with the Games

To help you find games suitable for a particular situation, all the games are coded with icons. These icons tell you at a glance some things about the game:

- the appropriate grade level/age group

- the amount of time needed

- the organization of the players

- the props required

- the space required

These are explained in more detail below.

Suitability in terms of age The age groups correspond to grade level divisions commonly used in the educational system:

   = Young children in kindergarten through grade 2 (ages 4 through 8)

 = Older children in grades 3 through 5 (ages 8 through 11)

 = Adolescents in middle school, grades 6 through 8 (ages 11 through 14)

= Teenagers in high school, grades 9 through 12 (ages 14 through 18)

= All ages

How long the game takes The games are divided into those that require about 10 minutes or less, 15 minutes, 30 minutes, 40 minutes or more, and those that require multiple class sessions.

10 minutes or less   15 minutes   30 minutes

40 minutes or more   multiple sessions

The organization of players All of the games can be adapted to virtually any size of group. The grouping icons indicate how players will be organized to play the game: in pairs, in small groups, as individuals, or all together as a group.

= Players will work in pairs.

 = Players will work in small groups.

 = Players will work as individuals.

 = All the players will work together as a group.

Amount of space needed An ordinary classroom is not suitable for most dance games. In general, you will need a larger and more open space, such as a gym. The games that require an especially large space are marked with the following icon.

 = Large space needed

Whether you need materials Most of the games require no special props or materials. In some cases props, scenery, audiovisual equipment, or other materials will enhance the game. These games are flagged with the following icon, and the necessary materials are listed next to the Materials heading:

 = Materials needed

Musical accompaniment Several games include suggestions for suitable music. For instance, we might recommend either rhythmic or restful music.

Introduction Dances

Players in a new group may feel self-conscious around each other. Since it's hard to dance when you're feeling self-conscious and uncertain, breaking the ice is important. Introduction dances are designed to help players get to know each other.

Dancing together is an interesting way to meet someone. Players may not find out right away where their fellow dancers are from or their likes and dislikes, but they get to know them in a different way. The information players convey to each other through dance is both more physical and more spiritual.

These games don't just introduce the players to each other; many also introduce basic elements of dance. You may want to avoid presenting these games to the group as *introduction dances*. If players know in advance that they are playing an introduction game, they will focus only on its social element. In these games, players learn to dance and get to know each other at the same time.

Think Fast!

♪ **Music:** "Sabre Dance" from Aram Khachaturian's *Gayane Suites* (or other fast music)

Have players spread out around the room. Play music and invite them to dance in place as fast as they can. Encourage players to move every part of their bodies—arms, fingers, elbows, legs, feet, head, hips, and so on. Tell them they should freeze when you give them the signal.

After players freeze, pick out a few players to demonstrate their moves while the others watch. Then have the group dance again, freeze them a second time, and pick new players to solo.

If players need inspiration, suggest themes for their movements. For example, you could invite players to pretend they are trying to avoid an invisible foe—players might stretch out and shrink down, flop down and grow upwards, bend and weave, sway and lurch back. Choose movements that suit the music. With younger groups, be sure to keep your suggestions simple.

How Slow Can You Go?

♪ **Music:** slow classical music (adagios)

Ask everyone to spread out. Tell players that in this game they will move as slowly as possible.

Start the music and invite players to begin moving in slow motion. Help them along by telling them to start with a single movement—perhaps slowly raising one arm. Keep suggesting new movements to make, until the whole body is in motion. The music should last for a few minutes. Remind players to keep their movements slow. You can use a few action words to suggest leisurely movements: *glide, float, amble, stretch,* and so on.

The **Tortoise** and the **Hare**

♪ **Music:** short musical selections, both fast and slow

This is an introduction game for forming pairs.

Ask everyone to spread out and start moving as soon as the music begins. Tell players to move quickly when the music is fast and slowly when the music is slow. Have them switch back and forth between fast and slow a few times. You can add to the fun by making abrupt, unexpected shifts from one tempo to the next and then back again.

Now freeze players in their positions. Have players pair up with the player nearest them. One partner will dance quickly, and the other will dance slowly. Challenge players to think up interesting ways of combining the two tempos. Will the fast partner dance in circles around the slow partner? Will the two partners do the same movements in different tempos? Have partners switch roles and play again.

How Strong Are You?

 Music: Music from movies—or no music at all

Games like arm wrestling and weight lifting are designed to show who has the greatest physical strength. The truth is that we are all strong and weak in different ways at different times. This dance isn't about winning; it's about working together. Everyone gets the chance to be strongest.

Divide the group into pairs. Tell them to move around the room together and make a series of poses. In each pose, one partner should act strong and powerful. The other partner should act weak and timid. Partners should switch roles with each pose. Their positions should fit together and complement each other. After a few minutes' practice, let each couple perform for the rest of the group to watch.

Tell players that their strong poses do not have to be high and their weak poses do not have to be low. The low crouch of a sumo wrestler is a very strong pose, and the droop of a tall willow tree could give an impression of weakness.

You will see some quite unusual combinations: The less strong children can now appear strong and vice versa.

What Do You Like to Do?

♪ **Music:** short musical selections with plenty of variety in tempo

Ask players to think of three activities they enjoy doing—for example: sprinting, jumping, diving. Give players a few minutes to practice acting out their activities in dance.

Encourage players to try dancing their activities in different sequences. Suggest that players try changing the level—dancing an activity up high or down low—to add variety to the dance.

Now let everyone sit down so they can watch the performances one by one.

6

Favorite Places

A favorite spot holds great emotional value for a person. Everyone feels safe and happy in their own place, wherever it may be. Ask players to create a dance about two of their favorite places: the sofa, their bed, a tree house, a jungle gym. Each dance must include at least two mimed actions to help the audience identify the places. For example, a player might mime sitting down on the sofa and curling up in the corner with a book. However, encourage players to dance and be creative in their movements—they shouldn't limit themselves to mime.

Give players a few minutes to practice and then invite each one to perform for the group. After each performance, encourage the group to guess what each place is.

Sleep Tight

♪ **Music:** soft, slow, "warm" music

Everyone has a favorite sleeping position: Do players lie on their backs, sides, or tummies to sleep? Do they like a fat pillow or a floppy one? How high do they pull up the covers?

Seat the group in a circle and have players come to the center one by one. Each player should show how he goes to sleep at night. Players can make a dance of pulling back the covers, snuggling into bed, and settling into their favorite position for sleep. If time allows, you could invite players to jump up from their sleep positions and do a short dance showing what they were dreaming about before they rejoin the circle.

Beginning and End

♪ **Music:** Music fragments of 20 to 30 seconds with a clear beginning and end. The music should have an emotional buildup. (Introductions to pieces of movie music are very good for this purpose.)

Play a piece of music for the group and ask them what kinds of feelings it evokes. Invite players to imagine this music is the soundtrack for a very short story, with a beginning, a middle, and an end. Ask players to create a dance showing what happens in the story. They should begin with a frozen pose that hints at an emotion. As the music plays, they should develop the events of their story. They can end their piece with another pose. Put the piece of music on "repeat" so that the players can hear when it is over and about to start again. Give players a few minutes to practice their dances, then invite them each to take turns performing for the group.

In advance, prepare a dance piece of your own to inspire players if necessary. You might use the example below. (If you do demonstrate the exercise yourself, you may want to have players create their dances to a different piece of music. Then they will not be unduly influenced by your example.)

Example:

a. starting pose: you are looking over your shoulder fearfully

b. development: you are running away; you trip and are captured

c. final pose: you are a prisoner in chains

Afterwards, discuss the ideas the players had. Encourage players to explain what was happening in their dances and how the music inspired them to think up the stories they created.

Silly Walks

 Music: humorous music

Everyone loves to laugh and be silly. Play funny music and invite players to spread out and make up silly walks. As players practice their walks, make suggestions, such as:

- Try walking up on your tiptoes or squatting down.

- Try taking big strides or baby steps.

- Is your walk so floppy that you keep falling over, or is it stiff and strong?

- Try walking faster or slower.

- Do you have just one way of walking, or do you change styles?

- What would be a good silly walk for a happy person? a miserable person? a vain person? Let the feelings show.

After players have walked around for a few minutes, choose a pair of players to approach each other. They greet each other when they meet, keeping in style with their special walks. Then invite all the players to walk around the room and greet each other "in character."

Who Leads the Dance?

 Music: background music (optional)

This is not simply an introduction dance, but also a cooperation dance. Everyone must work together to conceal the leader's identity.

Have players form a big circle and turn to their right. Choose a player to lead the group around in a counter-clockwise direction, dancing in any way she likes. The other players should watch the leader (or the player directly in front of them) and imitate her movements as they dance around the circle. Every time the leader changes her movements, encourage players to make the switch as quickly as they can. After the group has had a minute or two to practice, ask one player to wait outside the door until you call him.

Once that person has gone outside, silently choose a new leader for the circle to follow. Encourage players to conceal the leader's identity by avoiding staring at her and by imitating her movements as precisely as they can. Now call the player back in from outside the door and have him stand in the center of the circle while the rest of the group dance around him. He has three chances to guess who is leading the dance.

Variation: Have the leader dance in slow motion and freeze from time to time. This makes it just a little harder (but more fun) for everyone.

Copycat

♪ **Music:** slow music without pauses

Divide the group into pairs and have them spread out around the room. Partner A makes a few big, slow, sweeping, stretched-out movements. Partner B stands facing partner A and imitates these movements, but makes them smaller and more subtle—in miniature, as it were. If A stops, freezing the movement, B stops too.

Now ask partner A to watch while B copies A's dance, this time making the gestures just as big and sweeping as A did.

Then the roles are reversed: B makes wide movements and A follows in miniature. Afterwards, A presents all B's movements at full size while B observes.

The Room Is Shrinking!

Materials: chalk, traffic cones, benches, or another way to define the changing borders of the dance space

♪ **Music:** a piece that leads to a climax, such as Maurice Ravel's *Boléro*

Mark off a large dancing space with chalk, traffic cones, or long benches. Tell the group that you will play music and that the group members should dance inside the borders you have marked. Encourage players to use the whole space and make big, sweeping movements. The only rule is that they should avoid touching anyone. You can suggest some dance action words to help them along: *spin, jump, leap, reach up,* and *crouch down.*

As players dance, gradually make the dance space smaller and smaller by drawing a new chalk line or by moving the cones or benches inward. The object of the game is to make big movements in a shrinking space, while remaining aware of the other dancers at all times. How long can players keep moving without running into each other?

Body Dances

The joy of dancing has a lot to do with discovering and using new ways of moving. Body dances are dance games that focus on experimenting with movement. In these games, players try jumping, rolling, sliding, and moving in all sorts of unexpected ways. Players are encouraged to use their whole bodies and to make movements they have never thought of before. The emphasis here is not so much on creating a beautiful, expressive dance, but on exploring what players' bodies can do.

From Small to Large

♪ **Music:** classical music that evokes growth, such as Sergei Prokofiev's *Romeo and Juliet*

Ask players to spread out around the room and make themselves as small as possible. Have players freeze in their "small" poses, and start the music. As the music plays, invite players to begin to grow slowly, until they stretch their bodies to become as big as they can be.

Guide the actions from small to large and talk players through the exercise. Young children especially will find the actions easier if you suggest themes and images for them to picture as they move. For example, players might start as tiny seeds and grow into huge trees, or they might roll up like balls of wool and morph into towering basketball hoops. Start the music over and have players repeat the exercise a few times. For each new attempt, suggest new images. You might choose themes from children's stories involving growth, such as *Alice in Wonderland*.

Variations:

- Rather than staying in place, players could move around as they grow.

- Players could reverse the dance and go from big to small.

Cotton Candy

♪ **Music:** classical music with a slow melodic line, such as an adagio for strings

Invite players to imagine they just ate a big blob of cotton candy, the sticky pink spun-sugar treat sold at circuses and fairs. The candy got all over them, and now they are very sticky. Their feet are stuck to the floor, and if they touch a hand to their body, it will stick like glue. Encourage players to struggle to move in their new sticky state.

Play the music and invite players to try dancing. Point out that they can only dance slowly, and even that takes a lot of effort. Guide the players to improvise a slow dance that moves with great deliberation from one position to the next. Suggest movements and positions to players, and remind them how hard it is to move.

After a few minutes, have players move toward each other and form pairs who stick together to form one big blob of cotton candy. Partners form a single body, one piece of cotton candy that can stretch apart, squish back together, and so on. After a few minutes of practice, the couples can perform for the rest of the group.

Stop
Dance

♪ **Music:** different styles of music in short selections that you can switch on and off quickly

This game is a fun way to begin or end a dance session. It requires quick reactions to the music.

Play music, and invite players to dance. Tell them that when the music stops, they must freeze immediately, without changing their position. If one leg is in the air when the music stops, they should try to keep it there during the freeze. They can move as soon as the music starts again. (Make sure the pauses are only a few seconds long.)

If possible, play different styles of music in between each pause. Encourage players to match their dance moves to the music style. If the music is flowing, they should make smooth, flowing movements. If the music is bouncy, they should bounce. The choice of music will come as a surprise and help the children to learn different types of movements as well as training their reactions.

Reactions

♪ **Music:** soft background music or none at all

Have players stand in a straight line facing you. Before you begin, introduce a series of signals to the group. One clap means players should jump and get ready to move in whatever way you tell them. Two claps means they should freeze. Three claps means they should return to the starting line. Let players practice reacting to the signals a few times.

Now begin the game by clapping once. Call out a series of action words—*fall, leap, roll*—that players can perform in dance. Players should perform each action and move quickly to the next. Freeze players with two claps, then clap once more and begin another series. When players have moved forward far enough, clap three times to send them back to the starting line.

Movements in Isolation

♪ **Music:** repetitive staccato music (for example, tracks 2, 6, and 8 from the album *Tourist* by St. Germain)

In advance, practice making isolated movements. An isolated movement involves only one part of the body: an arm, a foot, or the head, for instance. Begin from a stationary position. Move just the part you've chosen in a quick, staccato motion, so that the part seems to shoot out from the body and back to its original position. Prepare a series of six isolated movements to demonstrate for the class.

Begin by showing the group what you mean by an isolated movement. Demonstrate the series you have practiced, showing the isolated movements following each other in succession.

Now ask everyone to find a place in the room. When the music starts, players should try out the series of isolated movements you demonstrated. Next, players can make up their own series of isolated movements and practice making them in quick succession. After players have had time to practice, invite them to perform for the group. Ask each player to perform her movement series twice.

Variation: You can let the group work in pairs and do the series as a relay. Partner A does one isolation and then freezes; partner B takes that movement over, does the next one, and freezes; partner A picks it up and does the following one; and so on.

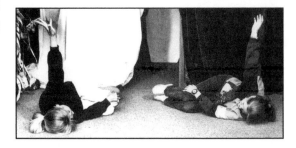

Memory Dance

♪ **Music:** repetitive staccato music (for example, tracks 2, 6, and 8 from the album *Tourist* by St. Germain)

This game is a sequel to game 17 (Movements in Isolation), and should be played in the following session. In game 17, you showed a series of isolated movements and asked players to repeat them. This game allows players to further develop their memory for movement.

Ask the group if they can still remember the series of movements they learned in game 17. Challenge them to repeat the movements without music. Then invite volunteers to add one or two movements to the series.

This short dance game can become a regular part of your class sessions. Have players line up and perform the series of movements simultaneously. In each session you can build up the series with new movements suggested by the players. This way you assemble a series of movements that don't really go together. The dance will be interesting to watch and challenging to remember. Testing the limits of what can be remembered is part of the fun!

Once the series is complete, it can be put to music. You can add to the challenge—and the fun—by choosing music that does not seem to match the movements.

Catapult

Materials: tumbling mats or a soft floor

♪ **Music:** fast, cheerful music

Let everyone find a space in the room where they can turn around freely without bumping into anyone else. Tell the players that this game is about finding all kinds of new ways of moving around. When the music starts, everyone makes quick movements down to the floor and back up again. The trick is that every movement upwards and downwards has to be completely different.

Next, invite players to imagine that they are kernels of corn in a pan over the fire. When the pan gets hot, they pop up. As soon as they come down, they should pop up again—the pan is too hot to touch for more than a moment. Encourage players to improvise their own styles for rolling around on the ground, popping up, and coming back down. Ask them to stay in roughly the same spots, to avoid colliding with their neighbors.

Now tell players to imagine themselves as projectiles being shot out from a catapult. Players should shoot themselves from one place to another. Encourage players to use their breath to help lend power to their catapult dance. They should dart off on the out breath, moving until their lungs are empty. When they have exhaled completely, they should come down to rest a moment as they breathe in. Then they can shoot themselves off again on the next exhalation.

Note: If necessary, you can alternate the high-tempo assignments with some relaxation exercises on the ground. Players can then catch their breath and calm down. If players are not in good physical condition, it is important to let them rest during the session.

Two Rolls

Materials: tumbling mats or a soft floor

This dance game is designed for rolling practice. In advance, think up two unusual ways of rolling that you can demonstrate to the group. You could use the examples below, or make up your own.

Roll 1: Lie down stretched out on your back. Now roll backwards over your left shoulder, stretching your left leg as you roll.

Roll 2: Lie on your stomach with your face turned to the left. Place your right hand on the ground and use it to push off. Begin the roll by tightening the stomach muscles. Then breathe out hard and raise your backside (as if someone is lifting you up from both sides of your pelvis). Your right arm will help you here. Roll over your left shoulder while keeping your legs straight.

Point out that you can roll in lots of different positions: with your legs together or apart, with one leg straight and the other bent, and so on. Now challenge each player to invent two new ways of rolling. After a few minutes of practice, let players show their rolls to the group.

Marionette

Materials: tumbling mats or a soft floor

♪ **Music:** dynamic music

In game 19 (Catapult), players explored using their breathing to lend power to their leaps across the room, and in game 20 (Two Rolls), players experimented with different techniques of rolling. This game combines the use of breath with the rolling movements and extends that use of breath to other movements.

Have players spread out and ask them what kinds of rolls they know how to do. Invite volunteers to show different rolls—backwards, forwards, sideways, and any other kind they can think of. Remind players to tuck their heads in and roll on their shoulders!

Guide players to use their breath consciously as they roll. Tell them to take a deep breath and then roll on the exhale, keeping it up until the breath is gone. Invite players to make a series of different rolls, always moving on the exhale and pausing on the inhale. Remind them to keep the movement relaxed. Encourage them to try to find new ways of rolling—using the arms or not or keeping the legs still or moving them (see photo sequence). Players can pause to watch each other for new ideas and then demonstrate the rolls they've discovered.

Now have players stand up and try jumping while thinking about their breath. Remind them to move on the exhale and pause on the inhale. Play the music and have players jump up and down, breathing out and in. Ask them to make their bodies completely floppy and relaxed, like puppets or rag dolls. Invite them to imagine, on the next exhale, that someone suddenly picks them up off the ground and then drops them again—they flop down, roll around, lie still, and breathe in. When they're ready to breathe out again, players can throw themselves back up into the air.

Rolling Music

Materials: tumbling mats or a soft floor

♪ **Music:** a short musical fragment (about 2 minutes long) that varies in tempo, dynamics, and intensity

Divide the group into pairs and ask them to create a dance in which rolling is the most important element. Let them listen to the music once. Explain that the dance should include forward rolls, backward rolls, side rolls, and any other variations players can come up with. Players may decide to portray an emotion or a story in their dance, or it could be completely abstract.

Give partners a minute or two to discuss the assignment. Tell the group that you will play the musical selection five times through while they create their dances. Point out that they will need to plan and try things out quickly. After about 10 minutes of practice, have pairs take turns presenting their dances to the whole group.

Creating a dance in a limited amount of time can be difficult at first. This creative method becomes much easier with regular practice.

Puzzle Pieces

♪ **Music:** music that varies in tempo and structure

In this game, players explore height levels. Have players form pairs. Explain that partners should link themselves together like puzzle pieces: Perhaps one can make himself tall and curve to the left, while the other can crouch low and hold her arms out in the space created by her partner's curve. As pairs dance around the room, they should vary their relative heights and their postures, but shift so that their positions fit together like the pieces of a puzzle. Partners will be constantly trading height levels. Tell them not to discuss the poses but to discover teamwork through improvisation.

Watch the pairs and make suggestions about how they can solve the body puzzles. Remind partners to keep switching back and forth between high and low.

Jumping
and Sliding

Materials: a springy, slippery floor (such as a wooden gymnasium floor); extra socks

♪ **Music:** rhythmic, staccato music (for jumping) and smooth, legato music (for sliding)—or one piece that incorporates both moods

This game is all about jumping and sliding. We spend most of our lives with our feet firmly planted on the ground. Jumping and sliding are great fun: They make us feel we are escaping reality for just a moment.

Before you begin, warm up the group with some stretching and calisthenics. Have them take off their shoes, leaving their socks on. (You might want to bring along a few extra pairs of athletic socks for any players who did not wear socks to class.) Ask players to spread out and then put the sliding music on. Invite them to slip and slide around the room. Players can skate around, using their arms for balance and momentum, swinging around the corner. They might get a running start and see how far they can skid. Encourage players to use their whole bodies in the sliding movement.

Next ask players to remove their socks. Play the jumping music and invite players to jump around, covering every inch of the room. Suggest that players try jumping like basketball players, like frogs, like kangaroos, like mountain goats. Invite them to see how high they can jump, how long they can jump, and how fast they can hop.

Now divide the group in two and have half the players put their socks back on. These players will be the sliders, and the barefoot players will be the jumpers. Play music—you might alternate jumping and sliding music, or find a piece that incorporates both moods. Ask the group to dance around the room. Jumpers and sliders can pair up and dance together as though playing hide-and-seek. A slider might crouch low and slide beneath a jumper's legs, leapfrog-style. A jumper might hop into a slider's track and hop along behind for a while. Have the jumpers and sliders switch places, and play the game again. If time allows, you might have jumper-and-slider pairs show their discoveries to the group.

Body Sailing

Materials: a springy, slippery floor (such as a wooden gymnasium floor)—not concrete; extra socks

♪ **Music:** smooth, legato music

This game is a sequel to game 24 (Jumping and Sliding) and can be played immediately afterwards. Of course, you can also play it independently. Before you begin, warm players up with stretching and calisthenics. Then ask players to remove their shoes, leaving their socks on. (You might want to bring along a few extra pairs of athletic socks for any players who did not wear socks to class.)

Have players space themselves along one wall of the room. Tell them that when the music starts, they should "sail" across the room without stopping. Encourage players to slide as far as they can before pushing off again. Ask them to travel in a straight line and avoid bumping into each other.

Next invite players to spread out around the room and sail toward any imaginary goal they choose. Players may cross paths, but they should watch where they are going and be careful not to injure anyone. Suggest that players vary their movements by adding sudden stops, twists, turns, and jumps.

Now have players imagine they are birds or airplanes flying in for a landing. Ask them to sail on, getting lower and lower until they come to a stop, sitting or lying on the ground. Then they can take off again.

Action Words

♪ **Music:** music with lots of contrast and effects, such as music from science fiction movies

Ask each player to think of two action words they can use in a dance—*wiggle, bounce, float, stomp,* or whatever they like. Then split the group into pairs. At the signal, the couples dance around the room, demonstrating their action words. The only rule is that the couple remain together while dancing, so they have to find ways of fitting together and still concentrating on their own words.

Now tell them that one member of each couple should dance on a high level, the other on a lower level. Ask how players' words can be danced on different levels. Players can switch levels as they go, but without discussion. Players should show with their body language that they are going to make a shift, and their partners should react accordingly. Encourage the dancers from the sidelines, suggesting new action words where necessary. Can partners manage to remain together yet always have one dancing high up and the other dancing down low?

Split the group in two and let one half dance as couples while the others watch to see what the dancers have discovered. Then let the second group dance.

pairs

Labyrinth

♪ **Music:** a one-minute selection of music with lots of contrast and effects, such as music from science fiction movies

In this game, pairs of players dance close together through an invisible labyrinth, with all kinds of obstacles at different levels. These obstacles are not fixed but seem to appear out of thin air and from every angle—so every couple has to maneuver to the side, over, underneath. Give pairs a few minutes to improvise in their imaginary labyrinth together.

Now invite pairs to create and rehearse a dance about a maze. Have partners give their dance a title and agree in advance what kind of a maze they want to portray. They will need to discuss and practice the path they will dance through the maze. Explain that the

dance should tell a story: Something interesting should happen in the maze. Are the dancers being chased? Does the maze cave in? Do they find treasure? Each couple should discuss the event it wants to show. Let the pairs rehearse for 10 minutes before showing their dances to the rest of the group.

Afterwards, you may want to have players make sketches of how the dance looked in their imagination. They could use these sketches to inspire ideas for a new version of the dance. Point out the open spaces in the drawings—how can they use that space next time?

Variation: You can also create a dancing maze. Some of the group (or the audience) can form two wiggly lines and dance, while the other couples dance their way through this "path." The path should be about 6 feet wide so that players have plenty of space to dance through. Once a couple has gone through the maze, the partners can become part of the pathway and let another couple dance through.

Object Dances

This series of games is a journey of discovery through the land of objects. Each game takes an object as its jumping-off point. Some of the games involve portraying an object in dance. The challenge of imitating something with a shape so different from the human shape forces players to be unusually inventive in their dancing.

Many more games involve dancing with props. Players explore the dance possibilities of ropes, balls, sheets, kitchen items, foam noodles, and more. The props described here may inspire you to try other objects, and that is terrific. However, not all objects lend themselves to dancing. Safety, of course, is always the most important concern. Objects that are heavy or sharp could pose a danger, and unwieldy objects may simply be frustrating to dance with. Practice using the objects yourself before presenting them to a group, to avoid disappointment.

Imaginary Jump Rope

♪ **Music:** music that is good for jumping, such as hip-hop music or a fast, rhythmic piano piece

Jumping rope has been popular with children for centuries. In that time, dozens of variations have been invented: One player may spin his own rope forwards or backwards, two players may spin a rope for a third to jump in many different ways, two players may spin two ropes for a third to jump (Double Dutch), or multiple players may jump at once. The jump rope games in this section (games 28–31) invite players to explore these variations and to create their own as well.

Have players stand in a circle and pretend they are jumping rope. Instruct them as follows:

- Jump from one foot to the other, as if you are exaggerating the action of walking in place. Bend the knees and consciously transfer the weight from one leg to the other, as if you're jumping rope. You don't have to hold your arms stiffly and mime holding a jump rope: You can let your arms dance loosely with the rhythm. Concentrate on the transfer of your weight.

- Now bounce around the room using exaggerated hops. Alternate large and small steps. Make your take-offs and landings easy to see.

- Try some sideways and backwards jumps—but look before you leap!

- Switch from jumping on two legs to jumping on one leg. Notice how the foot rolls from heel to toe as you prepare to jump up and back again when you land.

After practicing for a few minutes, everyone shows their jump-rope dance to the rest of the group, this time holding an imaginary rope. How many variations are there? Point out the different ways of bouncing and the different ways of using space.

Basic Jump Rope

Materials: individual jump ropes for each player

♪ **Music:** pop music with a simple structure, such as early Beatles songs

Hand out the jump ropes and invite players to spread out and practice using them. Put on some music that will inspire everyone to skip and improvise. Encourage players to explore different styles of jumping rope and different movements they can make while jumping. First have them do some simple exercises on one spot. Players might try crossing their arms over while turning the rope, jumping on one leg, swinging the rope from side to side, or turning the rope twice for each jump.

After a few minutes, invite them to jump around the room, varying the tempo, force, and level of their dance. They can also improvise their own special jumps. Suggest that players move in patterns—circles, figure eights, and so on. Encourage them to make their jumping into a dance by adding all kinds of variations and dance steps.

Have players form couples and stand facing each other. Ask partners to show each other the jumping variations they came up with, and to imitate each other's moves. Pairs can stand in one spot

at first and then move around the room together. Remind them that they take up more space when jumping rope than they do ordinarily. Players need to be especially careful to avoid hitting others with their ropes. Ask partners to come up with a jump rope dance for two.

If the group is large, you may need to split the group in two and have one half watch while the other half jumps. After they have all practiced for 10 minutes or so, let each couple perform their dance for all to see.

Sidewalk Jump Rope

Materials: one piece of light rope about 15 feet long for each group of three or more players

 Music: fast-moving music with a clearly defined beat

If necessary, call on three volunteers to help you demonstrate sidewalk-style jump rope. Have a volunteer hold each end of a length of rope. Teach the volunteers to turn the rope between them so that it moves at an even tempo, brushing the ground on the downswing and going a little over their heads on the upswing. Now show a third volunteer how to jump into the middle and hop each time the rope sweeps the ground.

Next, divide the group into teams of at least three players. Give a rope to each team and have the players take turns turning the rope, jumping in, hopping in place, and jumping out. Have them start out slowly and gradually increase the tempo to a nice, easy rhythm. Then ask players to improvise some tricks and dance steps as they jump:

- Have each player jump in, improvise eight special jumps in any style, and jump out again.

- Have players mime an action as they jump—running, swimming, going upstairs, and so on.

- Invite pairs of players to jump together. They can plan an action to mime together as they jump.

Finally, have the whole group line up next to one jump rope. As you turn the rope with a volunteer, tell a story that is full of action. You might tell a fairy tale, but an exciting adventure story may spur players on to greater heights. As players take turns jumping, they should act out your story in dance.

Double Dutch

Materials: individual jump ropes for each player, two 15-foot-long pieces of light rope for each group of about six players

♪ **Music:** fast-moving music with a clearly defined beat

Play music and let players warm up by jumping rope individually for a minute or two. Then divide the group into teams of about six players. Give each group two long jump ropes. Have one team help you demonstrate how to jump "Double Dutch." Two players should hold two ropes between them. Show them how to spin the ropes at the same time, turning first one and then the other toward the center, so that their paths interlock but the ropes never hit each other. Once the ropes are moving in an easy, regular rhythm, invite volunteers to try jumping into the middle and hopping over both ropes. Let all the teams practice this until they have the hang of it.

Now give the teams 20 minutes to come up with a dance using jump ropes. The dance can involve individual jump ropes, Double Dutch jumping, or a combination of the two. Encourage each team to create a pattern in space and come up with dance improvisations that can be done to the music while jumping. If necessary, inspire players with a few examples of your own. At the end of the 20 minutes, have teams perform for a minute or two in front of the group.

32

Imitating Paper

Materials: single sheets of paper

♪ **Music:** a piece involving tempo changes (for example, "Catacombs" from *Pictures at an Exhibition* by Modest Mussorgsky)

Display the sheet of paper to the group. Point out that paper can make all kinds of shapes and movements. Demonstrate by fanning the paper, letting it float to the floor, rolling it up, folding and unfolding it, scrunching it up into a ball, rolling it on the ground, and flattening it out again. Invite players to create a dance in which they portray a piece of paper with their own bodies.

Have players spread out around the room. Play the music and ask players to dance. You may want to inspire players (especially young children) by telling a story about the adventures of a sheet of

paper. Players act out what happens to the paper: Does someone take it out of an envelope and unfold it? Does someone crumple it and throw it away? Does it land softly and roll on the ground? Does it float away on the breeze?

The important things in this dance are concentration and inspiring background music. A dance game is a good exercise for letting the body experience new movements. After a few minutes, everyone can think of a series of paper shapes and make them into a dance. They can all perform their paper dances to the others if time allows.

Dancing Letters

Materials: newspapers and magazines with a variety of typefaces

♪ **Music:** background music (optional)

Kids don't have to sit at desks to learn the alphabet: They can dance the letters. Portraying letters through movement helps children recognize and remember letter shapes. In advance, cut out lots of big letters from newspapers and magazines and stick them on a white background so they can be clearly seen by everyone. Alternatively, you can simply write large capital letters on white paper.

Have players spread out and face you. Play music (if desired) and display one letter at a time. Challenge players to show each letter's shape in movement. Players might make the shape of a letter with their bodies, or they might move in a way that traces the letter's shape. If necessary, demonstrate a few letter dances yourself to inspire players.

Now have players pair up and form letters together. Encourage partners to cooperate and make sure they both form a part of each letter. Then have partners transform their letters into different letters. An *A* might morph into an *S*, for example. If time allows, pairs can perform their letter dances for the group.

Frozen Words

Materials: newspapers and magazines with a variety of typefaces

♪ **Music:** slow classical music with a constant atmosphere (for example, a nocturne by Frederic Chopin)

This game can be played as a sequel to game 33 (Dancing Letters). In advance, cut many large capital letters out of magazines and newspapers. Try to find letters in a wide variety of eye-catching typefaces. Combine letters in contrasting typefaces and glue them to white paper to form words with three to five letters.

First display the words and let players examine them. Then form teams of three to five players for each word—assign one letter to each team member. Give the groups 2 minutes to practice portraying their words. Each player should portray her letter by freezing as a statue in that letter's shape. Tell players to be very attentive to the shape of the letter and how they can show that with the body. Point out that letters have edges—rounded, straight, and so on. If necessary, demonstrate some ways of physically expressing letters.

When the teams are ready, have them present their words to the group. Team members should line up so that they spell the word starting at the audience's left. Challenge the group to guess the word portrayed, then ask the team to display its word on paper.

Dancing Photos

Materials: a series of dance photos cut from magazines and newspapers, showing a good variety of dance positions

♪ **Music:** slow classical music with a constant atmosphere (for example, a nocturne by Frederic Chopin)

Have the group sit in a circle. Display the photos and discuss them. Tell the group what dance form each picture shows—ballet, jazz,

modern, and so on. Point out how the dancers are standing or lying, where their balance is placed, what form is being depicted. How are the dancers holding their arms, legs, and torsos? What overall impression does each photo make?

Divide the group into teams and have each team work together to create a dance based on one of the pictures. After a few minutes of practice, have teams perform their "living photos." Freeze each team after a minute or so, and point out how each dance resembles the photo that inspired it.

Now have each team select two photos and create a dance that portrays one photo morphing into another. (Encourage teams to choose two contrasting forms of dance.) Teams should begin with a frozen tableau that represents one photo and dance the transition to the other photo, ending with another tableau. The whole dance should be done in slow motion so that the transition is very clear. When the teams are ready, let them present their living photos to the group.

36

Dancing with Pots and Pans

Materials: pots, pans, and other kitchen implements; large sheets of paper; thick felt pens; a cassette recorder with microphone and a blank tape

In this game, players compose a musical score, perform it using kitchen implements, record the music, and choreograph a dance to this accompaniment. This series of assignments can be done in two separate sessions or in a whole morning or afternoon. The subject of the piece of music and the dance will be a recipe gone wrong. A well-

equipped "kitchen" is essential for this game. In advance, bring in (or ask players to bring in) all manner of kitchen implements. Pots and pans, wooden and plastic spoons, eggbeaters, plastic bottles of water, even an oven rack—all make great musical instruments for accompanying the perfect recipe.

Skipping the list of ingredients, read out a recipe for pancakes or another simple, familiar food. Ask players to raise their hands whenever they hear an action (*beat, pour, fry...*) mentioned. For each action, call on a player to search the "kitchen" for the perfect implement to make that sound effect. The player might find the actual kitchen implement, or he might simulate the sound with another object—he could click two spoons together for the sound of eggs being cracked. In this way, everyone finds an instrument. You might also choose one or more players to keep a constant rhythm by drumming on a pot. Ask players to come up with something that goes wrong with the recipe. Does the pot boil over? Does the cook drop the pan? Players should come up with sound effects for the disaster as well.

Now write down the different actions for the recipe gone wrong on a large sheet of paper, leaving plenty of space. Above the words, draw pictures that indicate the sound effects players have chosen to represent those actions. Encourage players to make their composition build up to a climax and to give it a clear ending. You can use different colors to indicate dynamics and tone intensity (for example, red might mean "play as loud as possible"). When the score is complete, have players practice it and record it on tape.

Now that players have composed the music for their piece, they must choreograph the dance. Invite the group to portray the story of the recipe gone wrong through movement. Let players decide whether they want to use kitchen implements in their dance, or whether they would rather dance without props. Make sure all the players are included in the dance: Make suggestions for additional roles if necessary. Some players could be cooks, while others could be ingredients. Play the group's music several times through as the players practice their dance. Then have them perform, perhaps for another class or for their friends and family members.

Broccoli Dance

Materials: a piece of raw broccoli

♪ **Music:** a piece of music with two different accents, one for the hard, uncooked forms and one for the soft, cooked form

Have players spread out around the room. Display the piece of broccoli and let players study its shape and structure. Tell the group that they are uncooked broccoli: raw, hard, branching upward. Have them pose and move the way a piece of broccoli might. Are they stiff and formal in their movements? Are they unable to bend their knees?

Now tell players that they are cooking in a pot of water. Invite them to dance the transformation from raw to cooked. Encourage players to begin to relax in the bubbling water, letting their arms wave back and forth, gradually becoming more flexible. When players have finished cooking, they should be completely soft and floppy.

The dancers make a transition from a series of hard movement patterns to a series of soft ones. Point out that you need power and tension to make those changes in the body clearly visible. Split the group in two so one half can dance while the others watch. Then switch over.

Dance Your Favorite Food

♪ **Music:** music that makes you think of good food—perhaps Italian arias

This game could be played as a sequel to game 37 (Broccoli Dance). Ask players what they most like eating. Invite them to portray their favorite foods in dance. Explain that something should happen to their food in the dance: It could be cooked, chopped, or otherwise prepared. Alternatively, ice cream could melt, an egg could break, or a cookie could be eaten bit by bit.

Have players freeze in a starting pose that shows their favorite food before it is cooked or otherwise transformed. Then play music and invite them to bring the food to life. What happens to the shape? Does the food begin raw and hard and turn soft as it cooks? How can they show the food getting smaller and smaller as it is eaten? Ask players to move back and forth, from one state to the other (raw to cooked, frozen to melted, and so on). Encourage them to explore different tempos and height levels in their dance: Can they make the transformation faster or slower? Can the food move from high to low and back again? After 10 minutes of practice, invite players to present their dances to the group.

Dinner
for Two

♪ **Music:** *La Valse* by Maurice Ravel

Like game 37 (Broccoli Dance) and game 38 (Dance Your Favorite Food), this is a cooking dance. In this game, players pair up and focus on a small part of the cooking process. The game helps players increase their repertoire of movements. Imitating a specific (and changing) shape forces players to be inventive.

Each pair of players should choose a food that is transformed in the cooking process. Partners should then choose one part of the transformation to dance. For instance, if a pair chose scrambled eggs, they might dance the whisking step, in which yolk and white start out separate and are swirled together. Alternatively, they might choose the cooking step, in which the goopy egg mixture slowly solidifies into curds. Ask players to stick to one step in the process and work together to explore that transformation.

Play the music and invite players to dance. Encourage partners to react to each other, inspire each other, and collaborate. How can they work out the best way to show the food before it is transformed? What happens during the transformation? How do they end up?

After a few minutes, each couple can perform its dance to the music. As leader, you can clap to stop the improvisations so that they remain as brief impressions.

Dancing
with **Objects**

Materials: various large objects, such as a table, a broom, chairs, and so on

 Music: movie themes or classical music

Save this game until after players have participated in several dance sessions. Experienced players are accustomed to using their imagination to experiment with shapes.

Just before players arrive, arrange the objects in different spots in the middle of the dance space. You might stand some objects up and lay others upside down or on their sides. To begin the game, play music and invite players to dance around the objects in the room. Ask players not to touch the objects. Encourage them to observe how the objects divide the dance space. What movements do the objects prevent them from making? What new movements do they inspire?

Tell players the following:

Dance around the room and when you come across an object, skim past it. Take the contours of the object into account as you dance past it. Bend over it, dance under it, but still don't touch it. Try to keep to your trajectory across the room as if nothing were in the way. Be like a bird flying through or over a tree.

Now invite each player to choose one object around which to base a dance. Have everyone stand around the edges of the room, dancing in place or simply clapping to the music. Players should move forward one by one and perform their dances in relay: a series of solos for everyone to take part in and watch. Ask players to dance around, over, and under the object they choose. Encourage them to bring the object into their dance, without actually touching it.

Variation: Divide the group into smaller teams. Instead of arranging the objects yourself, invite one of the teams to place them around the room. A different team can use this arrangement to create a dance as above. Then the team that just finished dancing can rearrange the objects for another team to dance around. Repeat until all the teams have had a turn to dance and arrange the objects. How do the different arrangements influence the dances?

A Broom Is Your Dance Partner

Materials: various large objects, such as a table, a broom, chairs, and so on

♪ **Music:** percussion—African drumming, drum corps, and so on

In game 40 (Dancing with Objects), players danced around objects. This game makes objects an even more integral part of the dance: Now players can touch, climb on, and pick up the objects. This game can be played just after game 40 or on its own. Make sure the group has enough experience to be able to deal with abstract forms—this is a dance study in shapes.

Let players help you arrange the objects in the middle of the room. Encourage players to create a wild construction. Still, place the objects so that players can safely climb over and crawl under them: Make sure players don't stack anything precariously.

Play music and have players stand around the edges of the room. Invite them to shoot across the room one by one, choosing a high or low path around the objects. For the next turn, tell players they can touch the objects. Players might climb onto the construction and dance on top, slide down it and lie across a chair, or make a turn with the broom. Ask them to do a spontaneous dance with each object they come across. Encourage the dancers to go beyond using a broom to sweep: Ask them to consider more abstract, unusual movements they can make with the objects. Urge players to let the different shapes of the objects influence their dance. If they dance near a round object, they might make their bodies rounded and their movements fluid. If they dance near an angular object, they might make their bodies angular and their movements choppy.

As players dance, make suggestions from the sidelines:

- Is the object light or heavy?

- Is the object rounded or angular?

- Can you pick it up or push it around in your dance?

- Have you gone through it or under it from every angle?

If time allows, have each player create a one-minute dance using an object and perform it for the group. Encourage players to show how they experimented with new movements and uses for the object.

Foam Noodles

Materials: a foam "noodle" (commonly used as a swimming aide) for each player

♪ **Music:** new-age music or science fiction movie soundtracks, such as *The Matrix*

Large foam "noodles" are popular swimming aides. Many players may have one or more at home, or you may be able to borrow some from the school swimming pool. This material is extremely flexible, strong, nonthreatening (you couldn't hurt anyone with these noodles), and easy to obtain. Its flexibility makes it fantastic for use as a prop when you're dancing.

Before you hand out the noodles, display one to the group. Wave it, bend it, crush it together, and twist it to show its range of movement. Play music and invite players to spread out around the room and move like foam noodles. Tell the players to twist around, stretch out tall, wave back and forth, and then wind themselves downward until they are tucked up as small as they can be. Ask them to experiment with all kinds of new ways to move their bodies.

Now give everyone a noodle. Have players dance with the noodle, using both hands to guide it. What new kinds of movement does the noodle inspire? Encourage players to let the noodle take the lead in their dance and to imitate its shape and movements with their bodies. If the noodle is twisted, players should twist themselves too.

Next have players form pairs, one partner with a noodle and one without. The partner with the noodle guides the movements of the other. After a couple of minutes, have them switch roles and play again. Then let pairs dance with two noodles. Encourage partners to cooperate, experiment, imitate each other, and suggest new movements to each other. Finally, have pairs perform their noodle dances to the group. What new ways of dancing have players discovered by using the noodles?

Have a Ball

Materials: an easy-to-handle ball for each player, not too large and not too small

♪ **Music:** music with a consistent tempo created by a prominent bass or percussion beat

Hand out balls to players and put on the music. Invite players to dance while holding the balls. Encourage them to experiment with all the different ways they can move using the ball—twisting, spinning, leaping, rolling, moving from high to low, going fast or slowly. The only rule is that they should not let the ball drop.

Next have players pair up and pass one ball between them while dancing. Pairs should try to think up new ways to pass the ball back and forth—throwing, bouncing, handing it off behind the back or through the legs. Remind players not to drop the ball. Partners should stay together, but they can move all around the room.

Now give each pair two balls. Challenge them to keep both balls in the air. How long can they keep it up while dancing around the room to the music? After a few minutes, have the group stand around the edges of the dance space. Let each couple show its discoveries one after the other, like a relay team.

Giant Sheet

Materials: nine old double sheets stitched together to form a huge square (or a surplus parachute); spotlight (optional)

♪ **Music:** a symphony such as *Fratres* by Arvo Pärt

You can make some wonderful atmospheric dances in a darkened room with a spotlight on an almost transparent sheet (see photos on this and the next page)—but lighting effects are not essential. In advance, find a parachute at a surplus store or gather old sheets from players or thrift stores and stitch them together to form one giant square. Spread the sheet or parachute out on the floor.

Put the music on and crawl under the sheet to demonstrate its possibilities. Lie down so that you almost disappear under the sheet, then slowly grow upwards into a strange, draped form. Stick out your arms and legs under the sheet to transform yourself into all kinds of shapes. Shrink, disappear, and grow upward again. Then emerge and tell players they will have a turn to play with the sheet, too.

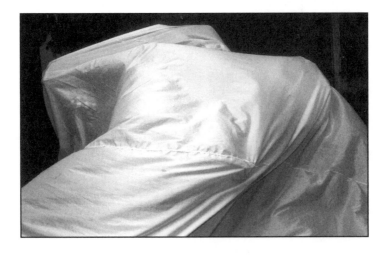

First have players practice outside the sheet. Have them form different shapes, big and small, with their bodies. Have them experiment with different slow dance steps they could try under the sheet later.

Now invite small groups of players to go under the sheet. Before each group disappears under the sheet, suggest an activity such as the ones below:

- Make yourself very small, then grow up until you are as tall as you can get, totally stretched out, then very slowly dance yourself back down into a little ball, so that no one could find you under the sheet.

- Lie down under the sheet and make yourself invisible. Come up in the strangest shape you can think of so that no one would guess it's a person. You might go upside down and stick one leg in the air, wiggle your arms so that the sheet shakes, or make a shape together with a friend.

- You find yourself in a cave... or an avalanche has buried you under the snow.... (You may wish to tell very young children a story to act out.)

Make sure all the players have a turn. The others can look at the shapes, remember them, and later draw them or make models from scrunched-up paper.

Story Dances

A story is the perfect way to start off a dance session for young children. At this age, abstract descriptions of movement styles and body positions can be confusing and uninteresting. You can inspire children by putting dance movements into the context of stories about nature and the seasons. The stories in these games do not necessarily have a beginning, middle, and end; rather, they are free-form exercises of the imagination. Players picture themselves as snowflakes, ocean waves, and even aliens from another planet. The stories open the door to exploration with movement in a uniquely accessible way.

You could adapt these games for teenagers by leaving out the story element and approaching the movement themes in a more abstract way. The experience will not be diminished.

It's Raining,
It's Pouring...

Rain is a lot of fun for little kids. They love to splash in the puddles in their boots. This game is based on the song "It's Raining, It's Pouring." The movements grow from the words into a dance.

Have players spread out and stretch. Encourage them to stretch as tall as they can, shrink back down, and stretch to one side and the other. Join in to demonstrate lots of different stretches. Then ask players to sit in a circle and sing "It's Raining, It's Pouring" twice through:

It's raining, it's pouring
The old man is snoring
He went to bed and bumped his head
And couldn't get up in the morning

Now have players stand up. Sing the song line by line, pausing to invite volunteers to think up a new movement to go with each line. For example:

It's raining . . . jump over the puddles

The old man . . . dance slowly and heavily

He went to bed . . . mime bumping your head as you dance

And couldn't get up . . . sink down slowly and lie relaxed on the floor

Sing the song two or three times all together as players dance the movements they thought up for each line. Then let players sing the song for themselves as they dance in any way they please. In the song the man bumps his head. But what other things happen when it's raining? Ask the children for their ideas. Encourage them to feel the raindrops falling and notice where all the puddles are. Small children love repetition, so feel free to let them sing the song many times over.

Raindrops

♪ **Music:** music that evokes rain, such as *Clair de Lune* by Claude Debussy

Raindrops make all kinds of interesting movements: They fall from the sky, splash into puddles, clatter against the windowpane, and stream down walls in rivulets.

Play the music and have players spread out. Explain that everyone is a raindrop, and players should drip, splash, and dribble around the room. They might roll, jump, and fall down again. If two raindrops collide, they will splash in opposite directions. Collisions must be very gentle—as players get close, they should be ready to leap backward.

Now line players up along the edge of the room. Have them cross the room diagonally in threes as groups of raindrops. On the other side, they drop individually into the "gutter" and dribble back to the end of the line. When they finish they should make a definite stop and freeze in position for a moment before the next three raindrops go off. The others watch and wait for their turn.

Finally, each player does a solo raindrop dance across the room. Each dance should tell a little story: Perhaps the raindrop is swallowed by the ocean or freezes into a snowflake.

Waves

♪ **Music:** environmental recordings of running water or music by Claude Debussy—especially *The Girl with the Flaxen Hair* and *Reverie*

From raindrop to wave is a logical step for a child. A huge wave is made up of tiny raindrops. For raindrops to grow into waves, players will need to cooperate.

Invite players to imagine they are raindrops falling from the sky and splashing into the ocean. Each player floats from one spot to the next. Encourage players to make little floating jumps forwards, sideways, at an angle, or backwards—every possible way—keeping down low near the ground. Then let them make bigger and bigger jumps, as if the seas are rising.

Tell players that if two of them meet up, they should dance together, keeping just a tiny space between them. Pair up players and rearrange pairings as necessary, until everyone has a partner. Partners can jump together and float across the room. They can also make waves together, perhaps by joining hands and undulating their arms, or by dancing together across the room, jumping high for the wave crests and diving low for the troughs. Encourage players to explore all the possibilities of being a wave.

Have each pair of players create a dance that tells the story of two raindrops that meet up and grow into a wave. Encourage them to think of lots of variations on this theme. After a few minutes of practice, have pairs perform their dances for the group.

Skating

Materials: a springy, slippery floor (such as a wooden gymnasium floor); extra socks

 Music: circus music or movie themes

This dance game has a winter theme, but it could refresh players in any season. Skating and dancing have a lot in common—there is even a sport called "ice dancing." In this game, players "skate" in their socks across a smooth floor. They experience skating as a dance full of beautiful movements and moments of perfect balance. This game is in four phases, and an entire dance session could be devoted to it. For an explanation of the phases of a dance session, see the introduction of this book.

Phase 1:

Ask players to take off their shoes, leaving their socks on. (You might want to bring along a few extra pairs of athletic socks for any players who did not wear socks to class.) Have them spread out and practice slipping and sliding around the room, as if their socks were ice skates. Encourage them to speed up and slow down, make sudden turns, and trace larger and smaller circles and swoops. Remind players to watch out for their neighbors.

Put the music on. Point out that figure skaters often dance with their arms as their legs propel them across the ice. Ask players to try making dance movements with their arms as they make bigger and bigger loops over the floor. Allow players to experiment for a while. Then encourage them to plan out a dance that will take them in broad sweeps around the room. Players can keep repeating the circuit, practicing and perfecting their moves. Suggest that they try stretching their arms out or pulling them in, letting their arms carry them higher and lower. Encourage them to make their skating an endlessly flowing movement, without any stops.

Phase 2:
Now have players skate around the room in pairs. One will be the leader and the other will follow close behind, the way speed skaters hang in the leader's wake. Encourage the followers to let the leaders' moves inspire them to come up with coordinating moves of their own, rather than simply imitating every move exactly. Have partners switch roles and skate again.

Stop the dance and line players up on opposite sides of the room, facing their partners. Have partners skate towards each other, slide past each other, and skate to the other side of the room. Have them do this several times, meeting and parting again in a different way each time. Partners might loop around each other, pass each other high or low, or even play leapfrog. Remind them to keep the movement flowing constantly—no stops!

Have players change partners and repeat phase 2.

Phase 3:
Have players work in pairs to plan and rehearse some figure-skating moves to music. Ask them to include moves they do together as well as ones they do individually. Encourage them to vary the tempo and force of the dance—one flourish can be wide and relaxed, followed by a more powerful twirl. Divide the group in half and let one half watch while the others practice.

Phase 4:
In this final phase the group is divided into teams of about four players. Tell players that they should work with their teammates to create a dance that tells a story about skating. They might tell the story of a skating competition or the story of a group of friends who skate on thin ice. For small children, a dance of skating animals is great fun; they love the idea of being an elephant or a giraffe on skates. Give teams 10 or 15 minutes to choreograph and practice their dances, and then ask them to perform for the others. Afterwards, players can discuss what they liked about other people's dances and ask questions about what they didn't understand.

Spring Dance

Materials: photos of flowers opening and closing (optional)

♪ **Music:** music that evokes springtime, such as "Spring" from Vivaldi's *Four Seasons*

This series of assignments is about the experience of spring and all that goes with it. Elements such as blossoms, young creatures, and fresh grass are all part of this. From their experience of spring, players put together a spring dance. This game is in four phases, and an entire dance session could be devoted to it. For an explanation of the phases of a dance session, see the introduction to this book.

Phase 1:
Discuss with players the way plants and trees bloom in the spring. The blossoms start as tightly closed buds and very slowly open their petals to become flowers. Show players photos of buds and flowers at different stages. Invite them to portray the blossoming process through dance. Players start curled up as tiny buds and, in slow motion, open into flowers. Players can dance this individually and then work in pairs. Each pair represents a flower and together they dance open and closed. When they close, they can put their arms around each other, then open their arms out again to let the flower open. There are many different ways of doing this: Encourage pairs to experiment.

Phase 2:
Have players spread out around the room. Tell them to imagine themselves in a spring meadow, with grass and flowers all around. Invite players to skip, roll, somersault, and creep through the meadow. Encourage players to try out new movements and combine them in ever-changing ways.

Next tell players to hunt for imaginary Easter eggs hidden in the meadow. Encourage them to make it clear from their dancing that they are searching for something and to show when they have found it. Players can search high and low, crouching down to the ground and craning to look into the crook of a tree.

Now warn players that the field is full of molehills—little mounds at the opening of a mole's tunnel. As players dance, they must hop over the molehills to avoid tripping or falling into them. After a while, players can dig in the ground like moles, traveling through winding tunnels, and coming up to the surface in different spots.

Phase 3:
Invite players to improvise a dance in which they portray different animals welcoming the spring. Remind them to use all the different ways of moving through the imaginary meadow that they explored in phase 2.

Phase 4:
Divide the group into fours and ask each team to think up a spring dance, rehearse it, and perform it. If necessary, first help players brainstorm about the things they see and experience in springtime. Point out that spring involves lots of changes, and encourage players to show changes in their dances. I once saw a dance in which a blossom fell from the tree and started to lead a life of its own. You can play music of about 1 minute in length to get things started. Afterwards let the dancers talk about their discoveries and how they used them.

Observation Dance

Music: a piece of music with surprising, exciting accents

♪ Lead players in a short discussion about observing nature. Do players like to take walks in the park and watch birds through binoculars or turn over stones to find bugs?

Invite players to imagine that they are aliens on a visit to observe Earth plants and animals. They are a kind of alien that is well suited to observation, because they have extra eyes all over their bodies: on their fingers, feet, elbows, and so on. Play the music and invite players to create a dance that shows these aliens on a walk through the woods. What do they decide to look at?

Point out that the eyes on different parts of dancers' bodies may have different ideas about what is interesting to observe. Is one hand stretching up to watch monkeys in the treetops, while the other scrutinizes ants on the forest floor? This stretching and tucking goes in all directions. Players' arms may want to go back and to the left but their legs have another idea in mind. The head goes one way and the torso another. Players' bodies will move in lots of different ways at the same time—high and low, fast and slow, with lots of power or very little. Stop the dance after a few minutes and have players discuss what the exercise was like and what they chose to observe.

Now have players work in pairs. Together, each couple forms a pair of binoculars that can see more than one thing at a time. In this dance partners need to hold hands and keep their balance while they stretch their bodies in different directions to observe different things. Divide the group in two and let one half do its dances to the music while the others watch. Encourage partners to show the audience what they are looking at through facial expressions and mimicry. If they are looking at fish, perhaps they will make fish mouths and blow bubbles. Remind partners that they must stay together—they are still a pair of binoculars.

Fall Dance

♪ **Music:** a piece of fast music, such as "Incantation" from the Cirque du Soleil soundtrack album *Quidam*

This guided dance fantasy is excellent for letting off steam when windy and stormy weather is making the children restless. Talk players through the dance.

Have players spread out around the room. Put the music on and tell them to make sure they are firmly planted on the ground because a strong wind is coming. Tell them: Watch out, here comes the wind! Stand firmly on the ground, but let your arms and body be blown in all directions. Remember to keep your roots in the ground.

Now ask players to freeze. Point to one player and tell her that the wind is blowing her away, all around the room. She should think

of leaves blowing in the wind—flying this way and that, swooping upwards, fluttering down again. After a few seconds, tell that player to freeze again. Choose another soloist to get blown around the room.

Snow Dance

Materials: tumbling mats or a soft floor

♪ **Music:** gentle piano music, such as "Innocence" or "Carousel" from the Cirque du Soleil soundtrack album *Quidam*

Save this game for a day when the weather is cold and windy outside and the room is deliciously warm and cozy. Have players spread out and find spots to lie down on their tummies, sides, or backs. Play the music softly. Speaking just loud enough so that players can hear you over the music, tell them to imagine they are snowflakes lying on the ground. Explain that the wind is beginning to blow, and they will drift and roll around on the ground. Remind players to be careful not to bump into each other. Suggest that, as they roll, the snowflakes grow into little snowballs. Ask players to show how their shape changes. If they meet up with another snowball, players can roll together. They may even want to link up and form one big snowball. What strange shapes can players form?

Now have players stand up and dance as snowflakes falling from the sky. Remind them that snowflakes tend to stick when they meet up. How will players link themselves together?

Party
Dance

Materials: art materials for making masks, such as construction paper, scissors, tape, string, markers, sequins or other small decorations, and glue

♪ **Music:** festive pieces of music with varying dynamics played in quick succession

Children love parties and there are plenty of excuses for throwing a party: birthdays, public holidays, special occasions, anniversaries, celebrations, and so on. Children learn a lot from these occasions. If you are supervising a dance group, you can turn an ordinary day into a party.

In an earlier session, have players make masks to use in the final dance. The masks could be any style, but cut extra-large eye holes so that players can see well enough to dance safely. Make sure that each mask fits comfortably over the head and won't slip—it needs to follow the head movements without getting in the way or falling off. The masks can represent clowns, animals, or whatever the children like. For children who are not accustomed to dancing, the disguise may help them to feel relaxed and more comfortable with dancing with other children (particularly those they don't know yet). This game has four phases. For an explanation of the phases of a dance session, see the introduction to this book.

Phase 1:
Warm players up with an introduction game (see page 12). Then have players spread out around the room and practice silly walks. Play the music and encourage players to make up the silliest walks they can. Ask them to change to a new walk every time you clap your hands. On occasion, give the group suggestions to try: Take mini

steps or giant strides, walk very slowly or very fast, raise your body up high or crouch low, and so on.

Tell players that if you touch them, they are frozen until you touch them again. Walk around and freeze various players for a minute or so at a time. While they are frozen, they can watch what the others are doing. Finally, have each player show his favorite walk to the group. The others can watch and then imitate each walk.

Phase 2:
Play a new piece of music and invite the group to dance. Tell them to imagine that the different parts of their bodies all have minds of their own and want to move in different ways and different directions. Maybe their arms want to go left, but their legs want to go right. Maybe their backs want to be stretched up high, but their heads want to be tucked down low. Call out action words to inspire children to move in different ways: *creep, prowl, roll, jump, tumble,* and so on.

Divide the group into pairs. Ask partners to take turns dancing and freezing. Partner A will begin dancing while partner B watches. Then A will freeze and B will dance her own dance. Encourage partners to switch back and forth frequently, inspiring each other to try out new ideas and carry on a dialog in dance.

Phase 3:

Have players change partners. Get out the masks and have one partner in each pair put on his mask. The masked partner will be the leader, and the other partner will follow him. Play some cheerful music. Dancing in a mask can be challenging, as even the best-designed mask limits visibility to some extent. For the sake of safety, the masked partners should first practice dancing quite slowly, trying out turns and twirls. The partners without masks should make sure their masked partners don't bump into anything.

After one minute, have partners change roles. Switching over several times from masked to unmasked and back trains players much more quickly than spending long periods in the same role. Call out suggestions from the sidelines—have players turn around, dance up high or down low, and so on. Tell players they should all freeze if you clap your hands. You can freeze players to prevent collisions. As players become accustomed to the masks, encourage them to increase the tempo of their dance and to experiment with different ways of moving.

Finally, invite everyone to put on a mask and dance independently.

Phase 4:

Form teams of four or five players each. Play a new piece of music about one minute in length. Tell players they will work with their teammates to create a masked dance to this music. Encourage teams to let their different masks influence the dance they create. A sun face will dance differently than a monster, which will dance differently than a monkey or clown. Players may wish to make up dances that tell a story about the characters their masks represent. Remind them to express emotions through the body, because no one can see their faces. Play the music about ten more times to give teams a chance to choreograph and practice their dances. Then invite each team to perform for the others.

Fairy Tale Ballet

♪ **Music:** ballet music, such as *The Sleeping Beauty* by Pyotr Il'yich Tchaikovsky

Tchaikovsky's ballet *The Sleeping Beauty* was inspired by the fairy tale of the same name. Invite players to turn a fairy tale into an improvised ballet of their own. You could choose almost any fairy tale. Play music and ask players to act out the story in dance as you tell it. Tell the fairy tale slowly, pausing after each action or emotion to give players time to express it in dance movements. Players don't need to play specific parts. Every player can dance every role, improvising the story in her own way.

Animal Dances

Observing the world of nature, we see myriad styles of movement, as different from each other as night and day. Jaguars, centipedes, octopuses, monkeys, fiddler crabs, and earthworms—they all move in fascinating and dramatically different ways. Animal motion can be an inspiring example for dance.

To move like an animal, you have to observe how it behaves—sleeping, eating, walking, playing. You can use nature films as an introduction to these games, but it's not essential. The games will help players to understand animals better and feel how differently animals move from humans (and from each other). The games include familiar animals as well as all sorts of amusing fantasy beasts. They can easily be adapted for any age group.

My Favorite Animal

♪ **Music:** music with animal associations such as the albums *Dance the Devil Away* by Outback, "Peter and the Wolf" by Sergei Prokofiev, *Birdy* by Peter Gabriel, and *Rhythm Hunter* by Brent Lewis

For children in kindergarten through grade 2:

Invite each player to tell what her favorite animal is. Encourage players to choose a variety of animals. If you end up with too many dogs, for instance, help players think of different breeds.

Play the music and ask players to become their favorite animals as they move around the room to the music. Encourage players to think hard about how that animal really moves. Point out that an elephant has a much heavier step than a giraffe.

Ask everyone to stop dancing and sit around the edges of the room. Have players choose another animal, without telling anyone what it is. One by one, players can come to the center and dance their new animal for the others to guess.

Variations for older children:

These are longer dance exercises and can be the subject of a separate session.

- As players dance their animals, encourage them to pair up with another animal that moves in similar ways.

- Group players together in teams of the same animal or animals with things in common—size, habitat, and so on. Groups might include dogs, farm animals, desert animals, very small animals, or animals that swim. Have the teams dance together.

- Instead of having players choose animals in advance, play different kinds of music and see what animals each piece suggests to the dancers.

- Divide the group into smaller teams and have them come up with a short story about animals to tell in a dance. For example, a dog surprises five cats lying on a wall. The cats dance high and low over various obstacles to escape. Give teams 5 minutes to practice, and then have them perform for the group.

56

Donkey-Duck

♪ **Music:** see suggestions for game 55 (My Favorite Animal)

Have players stand in a big circle. Dance like an animal and ask players to guess what animal you are. Then slowly change into a new animal. For example, the arm that imitates an elephant's swinging trunk might gradually change its motion to become a bird's flapping wing. Challenge the player to your right to dance your new animal, and then transform it into any animal he chooses. Go around the circle, asking each player to take over his neighbor's animal dance and slowly morph it into a new one.

On the second pass around the circle, invite players to add the animal sounds. The sound can be the last part of the animal to change, so that the bird trumpets like an elephant for a second before it begins chirping.

For the third round, dance as one animal but make the sound of another. Maybe you are eating grass like a donkey but quacking like a duck. The next one in the circle then takes over the movement and the sound. He changes first the movement—now it is a snake that quacks—and then the voice—now the snake is mooing! You can end up with barking rabbits, twittering tigers, and roaring mice.

Variation: Divide the group into pairs. Each pair has to create an animal that walks like one animal and talks like another. Players might invent the elephant-chicken, the donkey-duck, or the dog-monkey. Have pairs perform their animals, and challenge the group to guess what they are.

Group Animal

♪ **Music:** unusual, exciting music

Divide the group into teams of four or five. Each team should create an animal by joining themselves together in some way.

Tell teams to include every team member as a part of the animal. For example, two players might form an animal's legs, while two more players ride piggyback and form the animal's head and tail. Make sure players support each other safely. Once teams have formed their animals, ask them to work together to make movements typical of those animals.

After about 10 minutes of practice, put on music and let the animals dance for the rest of the group to admire.

58

Shadow Animals

Materials: a spotlight or strong work light and a large white sheet

The group is probably familiar with hand shadows—they may have used their hands to make shadows shaped like rabbits, dogs, ducks, and other animals. Invite them to try making big animal shadows with their whole bodies.

Seat players at one side of the room, facing the dance space. Bring the sheet out to the middle of the space. Have two volunteers hold up the top corners of the sheet while two others stretch the bottom corners down to form a screen. Darken the room and shine the lamp or spotlight on the screen from about 15 feet behind it.

Go behind the screen and show players how you can make shadows by standing between the light and the screen. Now invite players to come behind the screen one by one and dance as different animals. They can make the shapes of the animals, but encourage them to move like the animals, too. Make sure to rotate the screen holders, so that all the players have a turn.

Have players begin by portraying real animals. Once they get the hang of the game, invite players to invent fantasy animals. One member of the group can stand in front of the screen and comment on the action as if she were describing a rare animal in a zoo: "This is the only flassterpookis known to exist. They were thought to be extinct...." Players can have lots of fun with this.

If a screen is unavailable, project the shadows against a wall. Darken the rest of the room for a good effect.

Circus Animals

Materials: photos or videotapes of circus animals performing; tumbling mats or a soft floor

♪ **Music:** circus music such as the Cirque du Soleil soundtrack album *Quidam*

Show players photos or videos of circus animals in the middle of their act—perhaps a tiger jumping through a hoop or an elephant standing on three legs. Ask players to think about circus animals and the tricks they do and to choose one that really catches their imagination.

Put on the music. Have players choose spots in the room and get down on all fours, imitating the circus animals they have chosen. You will be the ringmaster, and they should wait in place for you to call out the tricks. Imitate a circus ringmaster as you tell players to

- Stand up on their hind legs and put their paws in the air (remember, this is a difficult trick for four-legged animals, and they might wobble).

- Balance on one leg.

- Roll over on their back.

- Jump in the air and roll when they come down.

- Find a partner and lean against each other in a balancing pose.

Now invite players to think up their own trick. Is there a jump or a difficult movement that only their animal could make, for instance an elephant on one leg waving his other feet in the air? Give players a few minutes to make up and practice their tricks. Now seat players in a circle and have them come to the center one by one to perform their tricks. Encourage seated players to help the performance along with lots of oohs and ahs and applause.

Character Dances

Our bodies are naturally expressive. We unconsciously communicate our emotions with our body language all the time. A dancer must learn to speak *consciously* with the body. Using the body to express a specific feeling or a character is one of the most difficult things to learn about dance.

This series of games helps players concentrate on the expressiveness of their dancing. The first few exercises are warm-ups designed to help players become more aware of their bodies. In the rest of the games, players portray characters and emotions through dance.

Seasoned dancers can feel whether the character or emotion they are trying to express is coming across right. For beginners, this can be harder to gauge. There may be underlying feelings that come through instead of those the dancer intends to convey. Once a group has gained some experience, you might want to let the players watch video recordings of themselves dancing. That way they can see the feeling of the dance as the audience experienced it.

Awareness

♪ **Music:** background music (optional)

Have players spread out around the room and guide them through some conscious warm-ups. Begin by loosening up the neck. Tell players:

- Move your head in slow circles, first turning to the left, then to the right.

- Hunch up your shoulders and drop them again.

- Wiggle your arms one after the other and then both together, until they feel completely loose.

- Draw circles in the air with both arms. Keep the movement going. Now reverse direction.

- Move your upper body around in circles. Now take the circular movement down to your hips.

- Pick up one leg and move it around in circles. Now rotate your leg just below the knee. Now take the circular movement down to your ankles, and then wiggle your toes. Do the same with the other leg.

- Lie down and wiggle your whole body. Now move your arms and legs in circles.

Invite players to move around the room while rotating various parts of their bodies. Encourage them to make big circles and small circles, close to the body and farther out. How do the circles move them around the room?

 **61**

Shake Yourself Loose

 Music: background music (optional)

Like game 60 (Awareness), this exercise helps increase players' consciousness of their bodies and movements. Have players stand in a circle and follow your movements as you give them the following commands:

- Rub your hand together.

- Wring your hands.

- Hold your arms out in front of you, palms up. Pretend you are juggling lots of balls. Flap your hands from the wrist joint up and down, side to side, around and around.

- Swing both arms up and down, back and forth. (This can be very relaxing for the shoulder muscles.) Keep your breathing slow and deep. Make the swings bigger and bigger. Now bend the knees as your arms go down, and straighten them as your arms come up again.

- Shake your whole body loose, throwing yourself up in the air. Make sure your whole body is relaxed, and don't force the movement.

Circle Dance

♪ **Music:** background music (optional)

Gather players in a circle and begin the game with a warm-up. Ask players to imitate you. Pat your hands down your whole body—start with your head and move down to your shoulders, arms, torso, thighs, knees, calves, and feet. Then stand straight again.

Have players spread out and make the circle as big as possible. Walk forward toward the center of the circle in a variety of styles and emotions:

- confidently, with big strides

- cautiously, on tiptoe

- miserably, hunched-over and shuffling

- angrily, stamping and clenching fists

- timidly alternating with toughly, taking faltering steps and then big strides

Have players imitate you and walk toward the center, then back up again for the next style of walk.

Start and Stop

It may sound obvious, but the most important parts of a dance are the beginning and the end. A dance should always start with a strong beginning posture and finish with a strong ending posture. This game helps make players aware of strong poses versus uninteresting ones. Players will learn how to start and stop a dance more consciously.

Have everyone spread out in a circle and imitate the postures you demonstrate. First assume a good, strong pose that uses space in an interesting way. By contrast, show players a weak, nondescript position, perhaps slouching and playing with your hair. Ask them which pose would be a more powerful way to start a dance. Demonstrate more poses for players to imitate, both strong and weak. Hold each posture for a moment before going on to the next one.

Now add emotions to the postures. Demonstrate pairs of contrasting poses: Start out swaggering and end up frightened; start out angry and end up conciliatory. Then invite players to come up with their own pairs of poses. Ask: Who can think of a good starting posture and a good ending posture? Who knows a cheerful starting position and a sad ending position? Let each player show her poses for the rest of the group to see and imitate.

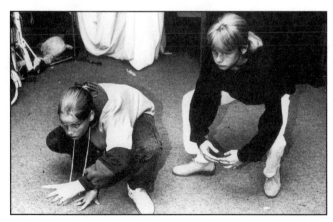

Dance of the Emotions

♪ **Music:** background music (optional)

It is easy to show an instant switch from one emotion to another—happy to sad, and so on. Making a slower transition between emotions can be more difficult.

Begin with abstract poses that do not evoke particular emotions. Have everyone spread out in a circle and imitate the poses you demonstrate. Take a starting pose, hold it for a moment, and gradually transform it until you freeze in a different ending posture. After you have led a few transitions, invite players to come up with their own poses. One after the other, players should think of and perform a transition. Everyone else copies them.

Now do the same exercise, but show a transition in feelings, for instance from angry to scared. The transformation should only take 5 seconds. Challenge players to think of different feelings and how they might be translated into dance. Players should try to find as many interesting transitions as possible.

whole group

One Feeling

 Music: music with one constant emotion, such as Chopin nocturnes—choose a piece that the group can relate to

This game is a sequel to game 64 (Dance of the Emotions). Now players have the opportunity to explore one emotion more deeply. This is a dance study and more suitable for experienced dancers.

Play the music while the players listen with eyes closed. Afterwards, have players discuss what feelings the piece brought forth for them.

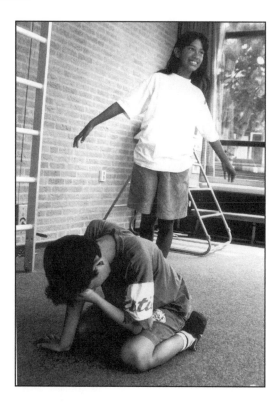

Have players find a space in the room. Play the music and let players dance. Ask them to have in mind a single feeling that they want to express through the body. This feeling should grow out of the music. Ask players to explore the movement possibilities the emotion offers and to deepen the emotion in their dance. Encourage the dancers from the sidelines with suggestions such as the following:

- Where do you want to start your dance, and where will you end up?

- Make the emotion visible in all parts of your body—arms, hands, legs, torso, face.

- Change the tempo of your dance; change your use of space (move high or low, use all parts of the room).

- Does the feeling remain constant or does the intensity of the feeling increase or decrease?

After 10 minutes, a few players can perform for the group. Save the rest of the performances for a later session. This will give you the chance to work seriously on individual development.

pairs

Dance Five Characters

🎵 **Music:** prepare a tape or CD with five short pieces of music expressing five different moods (cheerful, sad, creepy, romantic, and brave might be good choices)

Tell the group you will play music, and ask them to imagine that each piece is a different character's special theme song. Play each selection, and ask players what kind of person that music evokes. Is it an evil, scheming villain? Someone who is always just a bit too cheerful? A brave hero marching into battle?

Invite volunteers to dance to the first musical selection, portraying the character it evokes for them. Several dancers can show their vision of this character—each person will experience and portray the same mood in different ways. This is what makes the

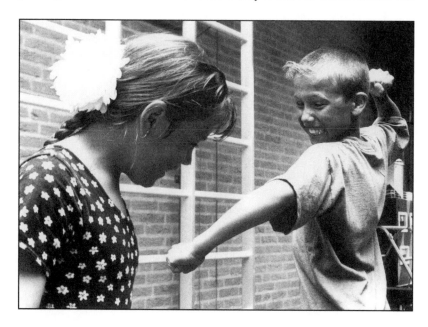

game so interesting. How can players express stubbornness, vanity, or treachery through dance? Encourage them to show the mood in the whole body—you may get some remarkable results!

Divide the group into pairs and have them sit down and listen to the music. Partners work out the details of the five characters they will dance, discussing their personalities and emotions. After 5 minutes of discussion, have players get up to dance. Partner A will lead the dance, with partner B following about 10 feet behind. Play the music and have all the A dancers dance each character while the B dancers imitate them. Ask players to freeze when each musical selection ends. As the next piece of music starts, they can unfreeze and dance the next character.

Play the series of musical selections again. This time the B dancers stand in front and decide how to portray each character. The A dancers follow along, imitating the B dancers. Afterwards, invite players to discuss how the interpretations differed.

The **Clown**

Materials: videotape or photos of clowns in action (optional)

♪ **Music:** circus music such as the Cirque du Soleil soundtrack album *Quidam*

Clowns train long and hard to be funny and bring audiences joy. Clowns are not just cheerful and funny, however. The figure of the sad clown can switch from comedy to tragedy and back at a moment's notice. Clowns can even seem frightening to many children. Professional clowns develop distinct characters and complicated routines.

Show the group a videotape or photos of clowns in action. Discuss the different characters: Are some clowns especially silly, bossy, sad, or affectionate? Invite players to choose their favorite clown, without telling anyone. Explain that they will perform as these clowns, and the others will try to guess which clowns they are.

Play the music and invite players to dance around as the clowns they chose. How does each clown move? Do the clowns skip, march, shuffle, or trip over their own feet? Call out feelings for the clowns to portray: sad, angry, excited, and so on. When players have the "feel" of that emotion in their bodies, go on to the next one. Also suggest changes in tempo, force, and use of space as players move around the room.

Now ask players to mime a specific action. For example, perhaps the clown decides to boil an egg. Point out that clowns exaggerate everything they do, moving very slowly and consciously, with lots of power behind the movements. Encourage players to make every gesture far grander than normal or necessary. For example, instead of an ordinary-sized egg, they might mime an egg as big as their hand—do they almost drop it? As players mime their actions, tell them that everything will go wrong when something unexpected happens. Perhaps the egg disappears, or a chick hatches out of it.

Give each player about 10 minutes to rehearse a clown performance. Ask them to tell the story of an action gone wrong in highly exaggerated mime. They should not use words or sounds. After each player performs, challenge the group to guess which clown personality that player chose.

Variation: Two clowns pair up—a smart one and a stupid one, of course, or a big one and a little one. Whatever one tries to do properly, the other messes up completely. Partners perform their dance stories for the group.

High-Wire Dance

♪ **Music:** movie music with lots of tension, such as the John Williams soundtracks for *The Empire Strikes Back* or *Raiders of the Lost Ark*

A tightrope walker needs to have nerves of steel. As he crosses the high wire, neither fear nor emotion can enter into his mind to send him off balance. In this game players set emotions aside in order to concentrate fully.

Have players spread out and find spaces where they have enough room to stretch out their arms to the sides. Put the music on and tell them to imagine they are tightrope walkers, balancing on a narrow rope high above the ground. Talk them through the exercise like this:

Start to move along your high wire with total concentration. Move your feet carefully, one in front of the other, along the rope. Shift your weight smoothly from one foot to the other. Slide your feet forward and slowly, deliberately, step forward, hold your balance, swing the other foot

around, and take the next step. Do this very gracefully, arms outstretched to keep your balance, back straight. Don't look at your feet. Keep your eyes on a fixed point in the distance and concentrate. Breathe deeply, keep your gaze fixed, and don't lose your concentration. If someone crosses your path, freeze on the spot until you can get your balance—don't fall! Keep yourself under control and show no emotion. Now begin to play more with the balance, taking some risks, perhaps raising your free leg in the air and holding a balancing pose.

Everyone can do this at the same time, each with his own high wire. One will go faster than another; one will use more wobbles. The important thing is that players keep in a straight line and don't disturb the concentration of the other players.

Split the group in two and let half of them demonstrate their high-wire dances while the others watch. Remind players: Concentrate; show no emotion; keep your body tense and straight; don't look at your feet; keep your balance.

Variation: Let just a few players walk the tightrope while others watch. This time, have the tightrope walkers close their eyes as they walk. Can they keep their balance? Do they stay in a straight line?

Echo Dance

🎵 **Music:** classical music involving theme and variation, such as *Symphony Number 3* by Sergei Prokofiev

Choreographers often call for a soloist to cross the stage in a certain way while a group of dancers follows. The group's movements might form a variation of the soloist's movements—they may echo the movements, repeat them numerous times, amplify them, or diminish them down to nothing.

In this dance game we will work on a composition with a dying echo. A soloist crosses the room first, followed after a moment by a group of dancers. The group echoes the soloist's movements, but with a little less energy, a little less emotion.

Choose a soloist who has a good enough repertoire of moves to be able to improvise without help. Put on the music and let everyone grow accustomed to it. The soloist takes up her pose and improvises to the music for less than one minute as the group watches. The improvisation should have a clear ending. Now let the soloist do her dance again. The others follow in a cluster, imitating the soloist's movements and emotion, but remaining part of the group.

Tell players to get ready to do the dance again, with the group imitating the soloist. Explain that this time, the group's dance should be a faint echo of the soloist's: It should have less power, emotion, and tension. How is the overall effect of the dying echo dance different from that of the first dance the group did together?

Split the class into three teams with three soloists. Have each team work together with its soloist to learn and perfect a dance. Each team of dancers should follow its soloist's movements in dying echo form. Each soloist should decide what emotion he wants to communicate in the dance. The soloist will express that emotion powerfully, while the group will express it more subtly. After 15 minutes of practice, have the teams perform their dances for the rest of the group.

Open-Air Dances

Devising a dance that works even better outside than inside is quite an art. In the open air, you feel more free, but also more exposed. You may feel small in the face of nature, but also connected to everything around you. You will see what fun is to be had dancing outside—on a field trip or the school playground, for a special performance or simply because it's a beautiful day.

The change of scenery alone will invigorate and inspire a group. Outdoor settings expand the possibilities for dance movements. Dancers can make use of whatever props they find all around them—trees, signs on the sidewalk, sand, leaves, and so on. Just as the outdoors can revitalize dancing, dancing can revitalize the outdoors. Even a familiar setting will feel new when the group experiences it through dance.

The five senses afford lots of inspiration, but can also disturb the concentration. If the air smells of spring flowers, players are more likely to do a merry dance than a sad or serious one. The important thing is to give assignments in quick succession to keep up the concentration, since there are so many distractions.

Your body feels smaller in a large, open space than in a room. Small, subtle movements will be lost out in the open, so players must scale their movements to match the setting. The first five games in this series help players prepare for outdoor work by enlarging their movements and exploring the concept of space.

In a public space, with strangers watching, dancers may feel quite self-conscious. Dressing up when working outside may help to diminish any uncomfortable feelings. Costumes, makeup, or masks can heighten the atmosphere and give dancers more courage.

A final note: Safety is, as always, the top priority. Whether you are working on grass, stone, or concrete, a fall can be painful. Watch carefully for broken glass and other sharp, dirty, or otherwise dangerous objects.

70

Enlargement

♪ **Music:** slow background music

This game is designed to prepare players for work outside. Subtle movements will be swallowed up in an open space: This game shows players how to make their movements big and sweeping.

Have players spread out and find a space. Demonstrate a simple dance gesture and repeat it several times. At first, keep the movement small; then make it grow larger and larger. A simple turn of the wrist, perhaps, becomes a larger circle, until it involves the whole arm. Choose a few different movements to enlarge in this way, and have players imitate you.

Next have players make up their own movements to enlarge. Ask each player to make one small movement—tap one foot, nod the head, wiggle a finger—and enlarge it over and over again, until it is as big as it can be.

Now divide the group into pairs. Partner A makes a gesture, and partner B enlarges it; partner A makes it bigger still, and partner B makes the final and largest gesture. Then have partners switch places and play again.

Everyday Dance

This game is designed to prepare players for work outside by exploring connections between everyday movements and dance.

Have players spread out and find a space. Ask everyone to think of an ordinary, everyday action that could be portrayed in mime, such as doing the dishes or taking a shower. Tell players that they will begin by miming that action realistically, and then they will exaggerate and enlarge the motion more and more until it becomes unrecognizable. (See game 70 for more practice with the concept of enlarging a movement.) The motion will transform from a realistic mime to an abstract dance. Demonstrate this yourself if players need an example.

Invite players to try going from mime to abstract dance and back again. Then ask players to organize their movements into five phases: from realistic mime; to a movement slightly exaggerated but still recognizable; to an even bigger movement, but still based on realism; to almost completely abstract movement; and finally to completely unrecognizable, abstract dance. Have them practice for a few minutes and remember the five steps.

Now have players begin with the final abstract gesture and transform it back to "reality." Suggest that they simply take the five phases in reverse order. Give players a few minutes to practice, and then have each one perform for the group. Challenge the group to guess what the action is before each player gets to the realistic mime phase. How many steps do they need to watch before guessing the action?

1,000 Dance Movements

♪ **Music:** movie themes (select two-minute fragments for the final performances)

This game should be rehearsed inside and performed outside.

Form a large circle and start with some basic warm-ups, such as game 60 (Awareness) and game 61 (Shake Yourself Loose). Now ask players to imitate you. Begin a movement with just one hand. Keep the arm still and see how much you can do with only the hand. Then add the lower arm—now you can move both elbow and wrist joints. Finally, add the upper arm, using the shoulder joint as well. Keep the tempo constant.

Now try the same exercise with both arms. Point out how simple movements of the arms and hands can turn into beautiful and interesting dance gestures. You can use the neck and head once the shoulder joints are in movement. Players will discover that they can make hundreds if not thousands of different dance gestures using only their arms, shoulders, and head.

Next, have players extend the movement down through their whole torsos. They can bend and twist at the waist, trying out all the dance gestures they can make with the upper half of their bodies. Invite players to begin dancing around slowly, moving in curves and circles while they make gestures with their upper bodies. The two halves of the body remain distinct: Players should keep the movements of their feet and legs simple, but keep experimenting with interesting upper-body movements. If dancers cross paths, they can react to each other: They might follow each other or dance in a pattern together. Ask them not to touch as they dance.

Now invite players to dance freely with their whole bodies. Encourage them to explore interesting and beautiful dance gestures that can be made with the lower part of the body. Ask them to dance on different levels, high and low, letting their movements flow.

Finally, divide the group into pairs and have them improvise together. Ask them to work out a dance that could be done outdoors. After 10 minutes of practice, take the group outside and have pairs dance.

73

Imaginary Street

Materials: props for dancing, such as hats, sunglasses, umbrellas, walking sticks, hoops, traffic cones

♪ **Music:** music with plenty of improvisations, such as tangos by Astor Piazzolla (choose pieces about 10 minutes long if possible, so players will become familiar with the music)

This game prepares players for dancing outside by letting them explore an imaginary public space. Have players spread out around the room. Then give them the following series of instructions:

- Swing your arms around to one side and back, to the other side, up and down. Try out all the different ways you can swing your arms.

- Move around the room as if you are being steered by someone with a remote control. Make sudden stops and changes of direction. Alternatively, you could imagine being blown along like a feather on the wind.

- Keep moving around the room, but now if you meet someone, you both make a sudden change of direction.

- Now imagine a street and buildings all around you. As you move, add different levels. Let your dance show that there are curbs, corners, bends, openings, and walls of different heights.

- Your street now has various starting/stopping places—like bus stops—that propel you from one spot a short distance to the next and so on.

- Pair up and take each other on tours of this imaginary street. As your partner leads you around, explore the place high and low—be drawn into the fantasy.

- Switch places with your partner so you both have a chance to see each other's city.

- Now find a new partner and explore the street again. (If time allows.)

Pause the dance and place various objects around the room (examples are listed under the Materials heading at the top of the previous page). Then ask players to dance again. Invite players to pick up objects as they dance and incorporate them into the game. Encourage them to try different ways of using the objects in the dance.

Finally, have teams of about four players perform the imaginary street dance while the rest of the group watches. Encourage players to think about what influence the different objects have on the use of space when dancing—an open umbrella involves a completely different use of space than a walking stick, for instance. The audience can give suggestions and make (positive) comments as well as getting new ideas themselves.

74

Chalk Lines

Materials: chalk for drawing on the floor; props for dancing, such as hats, sunglasses, umbrellas, walking sticks, hoops, traffic cones

♪ **Music:** repetitive music, such as movie music with long drawn-out themes

This game lets players explore the concept of space in preparation for dancing outside. Discuss with players the differences between outside and inside space. Brainstorm words that have to do with space and enclosure: *open, closed, cramped, cavernous, claustrophobic, wall, door, boundaries,* and so on. Talk about what it might be like to dance in different spaces, such as a phone booth, an empty football field, or a crowded sidewalk.

Now play the music and invite players to dance. Give them the following instructions:

- Take steps forward, backward, and sideways around the room. Imagine you can see your footprints. What kind of pattern are you making?

- As you make the footprints, begin to turn and swerve your upper body. Keep changing direction.

- Now crawl, roll, or slink along the floor, still switching direction all the time.

Stop the dance and hand out chalk. Have players help you draw random lines on the floor with chalk. Put some objects at the points where the lines cross. These same objects can later be used outside. When the space has been defined and decorated to your satisfaction, start the dance again. You may wish to have half the group dance while the other half watches. Inspire players as follows:

- Play with the space. Are the chalk lines paths you must move along or walls too high to scale? Dance along the lines or across them.

- You can enlarge or limit space as you dance. Imagine you are crawling through the cramped air ducts of a building. Imagine you are on a vast and empty plain. Imagine you are in a shop crammed with elaborate and delicate displays.

- Include the objects in your dance. Explore different ways to use them. Exaggerate your movements as you use the props. You may want to slow the dance down. Feel free to create a dance from whatever inspires you.

Ask the dancers what they have experienced that will help them when dancing in the open air, and where they would like to dance outside.

75

Dancing in a Field or Park

A large open space is ideal for bringing the concepts explored in games 70 through 74 outside. Dancing in an open, public space can be intimidating, especially when dancers are improvising informally rather than performing for an audience. Players may feel silly and self-conscious.

You may want to help players lose their self-consciousness and get them moving by beginning with a game of dance tag. Explain that this game is just like tag, except that players must move in a certain way—leaping, skipping, spinning, and so on. Choose one player to be "It." She should call out the style of movement and chase the others. When she tags another player, that player becomes the new "It." Each new player who is "It" can choose the style of movement for that round.

Once players are warmed up and ready to dance, have them perform the movements they practiced in game 70 (Enlargement), game 71 (Everyday Dance), or game 72 (1,000 Dance Movements). Alternatively, bring out the props players used in game 73 (Imaginary Street) or game 74 (Chalk Lines) and have players dance with those.

Dancing on the Beach

A field trip to the beach gives players the chance to dance in a completely different—and ever-changing—setting. In this game, players explore the texture of the sand and discover its possibilities as a dance surface. If the beach is fairly clean, players can dance barefoot. They can wear water shoes or sneakers if broken glass and other debris pose a threat.

First lead players down to the edge of the water. Have them spread out in a line and dance with the surf, creeping forward and leaping back, trying not to let the water touch their feet. You might add a rule that players who touch the water are out, and see who can stay in the game longest.

Next, have players dance from the firm, damp sand by the water's edge to the soft, dry sand farther up the beach. Ask them to dance back and forth from wet to dry, firm to soft. How does the soft, yielding sand affect their movements? Is it hard to move fast in the dry sand? Does it suck their feet in? Encourage players to explore the different movements they can make on a yielding surface, taking big steps and leaning way over.

Now ask players to work their feet into the soft sand until they are buried up to their ankles. Have them try making dance movements while firmly rooted in this way. You might have them imagine they are sea anemones, anchored to a rock but swaying in the waves. Players can experiment with drawing themselves in and reaching out, just as anemones do.

Divide the group into teams of about four players and have them create sand dances. Each team should choose an area of the beach as its stage. Teams might change the dance space by piling up sand hills or digging holes. Encourage them to use objects they find on the beach in their dance—big ropes of kelp, seashells, or driftwood, for instance. After about 10 minutes of practice, have teams perform for the group.

Dancing
in the **Woods**

A wooded area is a magical setting for dance. Woods have different possibilities and limitations, depending on how dense they are. If the underbrush is not too thick and you are free to wander off the path, you might use trees to create a unique dance set. Tie ropes between trees and hang sheets from the ropes. Arrange these curtains to form rooms to explore or a maze to dance through. Players might also explore the dance possibilities of climbing trees and swinging from branches.

However, many forests have thick underbrush, and in any case hikers are usually asked not to stray from the trail. This means that your dance may be confined to a linear path. Have players dance along the hiking trail. First you might ask them to dance on a high level, reaching up and enjoying the canopy overhead (but always being aware of roots and other hazards on the trail). Next players could dance slowly and down low, looking for bugs and other interesting features on the ground. A hiking trail is a perfect spot for a game of follow-the-leader. Players can take turns dancing at the front of the line, while the others follow along and imitate the leader's movements.

Finally, assign each player a spot along the trail, spaced at least several yards apart. If possible, each spot should have some sort of landmark associated with it—a big tree, a boulder, a fallen log. Have players explore their areas to find all the interesting features and possibilities for dance. Each player will have 10 minutes to create a short dance for his spot along the trail. Perhaps players will come up with a special sequence of stepping-stones across a stream, or a balancing act across a fallen log, or a place to duck in and out of a hollow tree. When players are ready, gather the whole group at one end of the trail and have them dance along it. Whenever the group reaches a player's spot, that player should take the lead, teaching the group her special dance for that spot. The others should copy the dance for that spot and continue to the next area.

Of course, players should wear hiking boots or sneakers for dancing in the woods. Long pants and sleeves are also advisable, especially in tick season.

Dancing
on a Hill

Virtually all indoor dance spaces share one common element: a level floor. Dancing outdoors on sloping ground opens up all kinds of new possibilities for movement. A grassy hill is ideal: You will need to adjust the activities if your area has been paved over.

Begin with some balancing moves near the foot of the hill. Have players stand sideways on the sloping ground, with one foot closer to the top of the hill and the other foot closer to the bottom. Challenge them to straighten their legs and balance so that they are standing as if the ground were flat. Invite players to experiment with other balancing moves and demonstrate them for other members of the group to try.

Then divide the group into pairs and have partners work together on balancing. First one player can stand farther up the hill and the other farther down the hill. Have them face each other, reach their palms out to each other, and lean together for support. Now challenge partners to shuffle their feet slowly backward, so that they are farther and farther apart on the hill. How does the slope affect their balance? Have partners switch positions and try the exercise again. Then let them try out their own balancing moves.

Next, ask players to dance up and down the hill. The first time you might have them run lightly up the hill, as if it's the easiest thing in the world. Then they might climb up in slow motion, as if they are struggling up Mount Everest. As players run down the hill, point out how momentum carries them faster and faster toward the bottom. Have players go up and down in many different ways: happily; fearfully, as if there's a monster at the top; on all fours; facing backward. Going up and down a hill is strenuous, so you may want to alternate this with restful activities, such as balancing. If the hill is very high, players don't have to run all the way to the top every time.

Now invite players to lie sideways at the top of the hill and log-roll down to the bottom. Players can experiment with different ways of rolling down the hill. They can even try rolling up the hill, at least a little ways. Have them stand at the bottom of the hill facing up, and ask them to do a forward somersault uphill. They should end up lying on their backs with their feet pointing to the top of the hill.

Have players pair up again. Ask partners to create a dance in which one of them starts at the top of the hill and the other starts at the bottom. Encourage them to think about the way the hill affects their momentum, balance, and movement, and to take advantage of those effects in their dance. After 10 minutes of practice, invite pairs to perform for the group.

Dancing in the Playground

The playground is a readily available, safe outdoor space where players can explore dancing with objects. As leader, your challenge is to get players to look beyond the proscribed uses of each piece of playground equipment. Encourage them to dance with the equipment and use it in unusual ways. Instead of just climbing up a ladder, sitting down on the slide, and sliding to the bottom, players might slither up the slide and slowly slip back down it, lying on their tummies. What kind of dance could they do with their legs while flying through the air on a swing? How might a monkey dance while swinging on the monkey bars? Of course, safety is always a primary concern: Keep an eye on players to make sure they don't try dangerous tricks.

Have the group work together to make up a circuit around the playground. They should decide in what order they want to dance on the pieces of equipment, and they should choose a path from one piece to the next. Then players can dance around the circuit, improvising moves on each piece of equipment in turn. Finally, have each player choose her favorite piece of equipment and perform a short dance on it for the whole group.

Variation: Many playgrounds include blacktop where you can mark out play areas with chalk. These are good spaces for traditional sidewalk games such as hopscotch. You could also play an outdoor version of game 74 (Chalk Lines).

Painting Dances

Visual artists use line, color, form, and texture to express themselves. Dancers use their bodies as a means of expression; they communicate what they want to say through movement and gesture. The dancer's body is his sculpture; the pattern he traces on the stage is his painting.

Everyone knows that music makes you want to dance, but could a sculpture, a painting, or a photograph in the newspaper also inspire a dance? The dance games in this series take the visual arts as their starting point. In some of the games, players create dances inspired by the poses of statues or figures in paintings. In others, the body becomes a brush and traces the lines of a painting in the air, using movement to suggest color and form.

Having Your Fling

♪ **Music:** dynamic music, such as *Rodeo* by Aaron Copland or selections from *West Side Story* by Leonard Bernstein

The group may be familiar with the game of crack-the-whip, in which a line of players join hands and run side by side. When the player at one end of the line stops short, the player at the other end is flung across the field by the force of momentum. Tell players that in this game, they will fling themselves around from one position to the next.

Ask players to spread out around the room. Play the music and invite players to throw themselves into the air and float down again on the same spot. When they come down, players should freeze in whatever pose their bodies fall into naturally.

Next have players line up along one side of the room and spread out, then fling themselves across the room. Ask them to move straight ahead and to avoid collisions with their neighbors. Each time players come down, they should freeze in their poses. Then they can get up for the next fling. As players fling themselves across the room, give them ideas on how to vary the dance by moving higher or lower, slower or faster.

Finally, let players fling themselves across the room one by one. This way everyone can see the different variations.

81

Dance the Painting

Materials: photos of artwork showing people in unusual and varied positions—perhaps statues by Auguste Rodin or paintings by Hieronymus Bosch, Pablo Picasso, or Salvador Dalí; paper and pens

♪ **Music:** alternately fast and slow music

Display the images and have each player choose a work of art. Tell players they will create dances inspired by the art. Before they begin choreographing, have players think about the emotions and ideas the artwork they chose evokes for them. Ask them to list these feelings and ideas on paper.

Now play music and invite players to begin choreographing their dances. They might base the movements of their dance on the positions of people in the artworks. They might tell a story about the artwork in dance. Players should keep their images and lists of words handy at the side of the room so that they can refresh their memories or add new words as they rehearse.

After about 20 minutes of practice, tape players' images to the wall. Ask them to guide you on a tour of their art collection. As you point to each image, the player who chose it should bring it to life through dance.

Variation: Experienced players might dance a painting from figurative to abstract. Include abstract portraits by Picasso and others in your collection of prints. Have players choose a "realistic" figurative painting and a painting that is more abstract. They choose a figure from a realistic painting and begin their dance from that figure's pose. As the dance goes on, it gradually changes to become increasingly abstract. Players' movements and body positions will begin to look less and less like natural human poses and gestures.

Art Morph

Materials: photos of paintings and sculptures that show interesting body positions, such as *The Gleaners* by Jean-François Millet

♪ **Music:** atmospheric background music (optional)

This is a sequel to game 81 (Dance the Painting), but it could also be played independently.

Have players form pairs. Each pair should pick out four works of art. Explain that each pair will create a dance in which one work of art morphs into another, which morphs into the next, and so on.

Suggest that partners begin practicing by studying the images they chose and copying the poses shown in each one until they can easily freeze in those poses. Then partners can practice dancing the transition from one picture to the next. This can be done by slowing the dance down and letting one frozen pose gradually transform into the next one. You can add music here if it will help, but it is not essential.

After 10 minutes of practice, have pairs perform for the group. Ask them to display the works of art they chose first, and then perform their four-part exhibition. After the performances are completed, the whole group can discuss what they saw and experienced.

Art
Gallery

 Music: atmospheric background music (optional)

This is a game for training the ability to concentrate.

Split the group into two roughly equal teams. Tell players that they will be statues, and assign one member of each team to be the sculptor.

Have one team dance while the other team watches. Let the statues dance freely for a minute, then clap your hands to make them freeze. Now the sculptor goes to work. She visits each statue in turn and molds it to create a dance pose portraying a theme—it could be anything from "Friendship" to "The Football Player" to "The Lion Caged." The statue should also express an emotion—happiness, fear, anger, and so on. Ask the sculptor to stretch and bend the statues' limbs into the desired pose very slowly and gently. If necessary, the sculptor can speak to the statue to explain what she is trying to achieve.

Encourage the sculptor to create poses that capture movement, rather than static poses. Suggest that players think of the poses as a frozen moment of a dance. The statues need to aware of this as much as the sculptor.

After 5 minutes one team makes its presentation and the others walk around as if in a gallery. The sculptors guide the spectators through the gallery, tell each statue's title, and talk about the subject of each one. Then have the teams switch roles.

Group Portrait

Materials: prints of Rembrandt's *Night Watch* and other paintings showing groups of people; perhaps some pieces of cloth and household objects

 Music: atmospheric background music (optional)

Divide the group into teams of about four players. Show the teams prints of group portraits, or of genre or history paintings—paintings that show groups of people in action. Have teams imitate the poses in the paintings. Teams can use props and pieces of cloth to help create their *tableaux vivants* of the paintings.

Now ask the teams to create their own original group portraits. Players should pose together so that they form an interesting, unified scene. You can prompt them with questions such as "What kind of group is this? Are these people a family? Do they work together? Are they living today or long ago? Is the portrait posed formally? Does it show an action frozen in time?" and so on.

As teams practice their tableaux, ask them about the emotions they are trying to express and give them suggestions about poses and facial expressions. Make your comments quietly to avoid breaking players' concentration.

When teams are ready, have them perform their portraits for the group. Team members should dance in slow motion into their positions and freeze. Give the group a chance to study the portrait for a while. Then give the signal for the portrait to break up. The scene slowly melts as the players dance their theme away in slow motion until they rejoin the audience.

Dancing Statues

♪ **Music:** lively music

Tell players they will be both statue and sculptor in this game.

Have players line up on one side of the room. Play the music and ask the first player to dance forward and freeze into a statue pose. The next player should dance into a complementary position and freeze. Two more players can then come forward and complete the effect.

Now explain that each time a new statue is added, one of the original statues should unfreeze and dance back to the side of the room. Players can only leave one at a time.

Each new player who dances into the statue garden can weave in and out among the frozen statues before choosing a space and a pose. The more statues there are on display, the more intricate the dances can become as the statues wind their way into place.

Encourage players to choose statue poses that complement each other. As players enter and exit, the tableau will be continually evolving.

You may want to stop the game occasionally to point out interesting groupings. Discuss the combination of stillness and movement that characterizes this game. How is this dance different from a dance in which everyone is in constant movement?

You Are a Paintbrush

Materials: posters, prints, or postcards of paintings

♪ **Music:** Modest Mussorgsky's *Pictures at an Exhibition*, Sergei Prokofiev's *Romeo and Juliet*, Igor Stravinsky's *Firebird* or *Rite of Spring*

In advance, tape posters, prints, and postcards of paintings on the wall around the room. Tell players that their bodies are paintbrushes, and invite them to paint the air around them. Players can experiment with long, sweeping brushstrokes, delicate feathery strokes, or pointillist spots of paint. First players can use their hands as the paintbrush, then their feet, or their backs. They might try painting across the floor. Encourage them to vary the tempo of their movements.

Ask players what colors they are painting. Encourage them to use their bodies to show the different colors. Perhaps they will dance with more energy and power if they are painting a bright color; they might make softer movements for a pale color and heavier movements for a dark color. Ask volunteers to paint shapes in the air, one by one. Challenge the group to guess what is being painted and what color it is.

Now have each player choose a painting from the prints on the wall. Invite players to use their bodies to paint the paintings they chose. As they brush in the lines and forms of the paintings, remind them to use the intensity of their dance to show the different colors. Tell them they don't need to paint every object in the painting or put every brushstroke in its proper place.

Divide the group into teams of about four players. Each team has 15 minutes to prepare a dance of a painting of their choice. While the teams are rehearsing, go around to encourage them and make suggestions. Help players to understand the atmosphere of the painting they chose so they can express that in their dance. Ask them about the feelings it evokes and its different colors, shapes, masses, and spaces. Encourage them to think about how they can make it clear what they are depicting. Ask them where the first brushstroke should go and how the painting will develop. Will each team member paint a different area of the canvas? Will they each choose a color instead? When teams are ready, have them perform for the group. Challenge the group to identify the painting each team has chosen.

Dance Maps

Describing the steps of a dance in words can be quite difficult. For example, if a choreographer calls for partners to "touch your palms together," does she mean that each dancer should hold his hands with palms together in a prayer position or that the dancers should hold out their hands to each other and touch palms? It is much simpler and more accurate to show a dance than to describe it.

But people cannot remember a dance forever. Many ancient dances have been lost to us because no one is left to show how the steps were danced. In order to record dances for posterity, choreographers have invented various dance notation systems. These are complicated marks that represent different parts of the body, their positions, and how they move. Today, dance companies use a combination of video and dance notation to record the steps of their dances.

In the following games, players draw maps and symbols to represent dances of their own. The games might inspire players to come up with other notation systems. For example, they might make sketches in boxes to show where the dancers are at different stages of the dance and the paths they follow to go from one point to the next. In each subsequent square players can draw what changes in the situation. It may take 30 squares to draw the whole dance.

Roller Coaster

Materials: large sheets of paper and drawing pencils

♪ **Music:** exciting music to inspire the dancers

First Session:
Invite players to design their own roller coasters. Have them map the roller coasters on paper, from a bird's eye view. Encourage players to take up the entire sheet with their drawings, including lots of twists and turns in the coaster's trajectory. Players might use color to indicate the high and low points of the track.

Explain that players will dance these roller coasters. Ask each player to walk through her roller coaster plan. As players do so, have them write action words on their maps, noting where a dancer should speed up, float, crouch down, and so on. Ask players to draw or write everything a dancer would need to know in order to dance this roller coaster.

Second Session:
Divide the group into teams of about four players. Each team member in turn demonstrates his dance to the others. Then he displays the roller coaster map and teaches them the different steps of his pattern.

Teams should practice each member's dance together. To perform the dances, have players stand in a line with their hands on the shoulders of the player in front of them. They will be linked like the cars of a roller coaster. Each team member can lead the chain for the dance through his own roller coaster pattern. When the teams are ready, have them perform for the rest of the group.

You can also mix the groups up and repeat the exercise, so that everyone gets to learn more patterns. Afterwards, hang all the dance maps on the wall so everyone can see how they are designed and drawn.

Haunted House

Materials: large sheets of paper and drawing pencils

♪ **Music:** spooky, exciting music (a selection about 3 minutes long)

First Session:
Play the music and ask players what kinds of spooky happenings it evokes. Invite players to work in teams of about six players to create their own haunted houses. Explain that teams will design a path through a house with different rooms, each one filled with scary surprises. They will later guide visitors on a tour of the house, accompanied by the music.

Each team should choose one player to be the tour guide. The other players will create the spooky atmosphere and surprises. Have teams draw out a floor plan for the haunted house, planning out a path for visitors and including all kinds of dance tricks. Will great big spiders suddenly pop up in the kitchen? Are the houseplants huge, hungry Venus's-flytraps? Players can practice their tour and draw their plan at the same time, making notes and changes as they go along.

Ask teams to include at least five rooms or situations in their tour. Encourage teams to vary the level of tension: Some surprises could be just little shocks; some could be *really* scary! There should be surprising, unexpected changes in environment—places visitors have to crawl through, bottomless pits to inch around, puddles of slime, and so on. The house maps should describe all the details of the rooms and also tell what dance movements the spooky creatures found there will make: scuttle, float, reach out menacingly, and so on. Players should make a note of the order the dance movements should come in, remembering to include plenty of variety in height levels, tempo, and power.

Point out that the dancers who inhabit the haunted house can move from place to place as the visitors are guided through. Ask teams to plan the dancers' positions during the tour and practice the timing. The guide can regulate the speed of the tour to make sure the other dancers have time to take up their new positions. The guide may want to write down interesting facts to tell visitors: Who lived here? What happened to them? What spirits haunt the house now? This will give the other dancers a chance to prepare the next surprise.

Second Session:
Give teams a few minutes for a final rehearsal and review of their plans. Then have each team guide the rest of the group on tours through their haunted houses. Afterwards, display the house plans and have players discuss how teams recorded their dance ideas.

Musical Dances

Music and dance seem to be inseparable. How can you dance without music? And what would music be without all the thousands of dance forms that have come into being over the ages?

Usually the music comes first, and it inspires the dance. This series of games turns the tables. The games give players the chance to make their own music as they dance. Players sing, rap, play instruments, and make strange noises using their voices or common household objects. Dancing to their own musical accompaniment, they explore the relationship between sound and dance.

Dance of Sounds

Gather players into a circle. Demonstrate various sounds you can make with the voice and body and let everyone follow suit. You might make short, sharp shouts, long, slow wails, claps, whistles, thumps (by hitting your chest, tummy, and knees with your hands), and so on. Point out all the different possibilities and let the group try them out so that the players become aware of their huge vocabulary of sound. This is also a good warm-up for the voice.

Now have players spread out around the room. Tell players that they will each create a series of sounds and a series of dance movements that go with them. For example, players might make a soft whistling noise and float around the room to it. They might make sharp, staccato sounds and dance with choppy motions to this accompaniment. Encourage them to match the movement to the sound: If the sounds are quick, the movements should be, too. Encourage players to observe and inspire each other. Point out that there is more than one sound that could work with a particular movement, and vice versa.

Ask each player to try to come up with at least a couple of sound/movement combinations. When everyone is ready, bring players back into a circle and let each one in turn show what he has created.

Musical Objects

Materials: various large objects, such as a table, a broom, chairs, and so on

 Music: voices, percussion with hands and feet

This game combines elements from game 40 (Dancing with Objects), game 41 (A Broom Is Your Dance Partner), and game 89 (Dance of Sounds). Players dance with objects and accompany themselves by vocalizing and using the objects as percussion instruments. In preparation for this game, have the group play games 40 and 41 in an earlier session. Play game 89 just before you begin this game, to loosen up the vocal cords and introduce the concept of dancing while making sounds.

Ask players to help you place the objects in various spots around the room. Now invite them to continue exploring sound/movement combinations (as they did in game 89). This time, however, their dance will include the objects in the room. As players dance around, over, under, and through the objects, they should use their voices to accompany the dance. Let players practice for a few minutes.

Now add a new wrinkle: Invite players to use the objects as instruments. Whenever players come to an object, they can drum on it with their hands, knock it with their feet, slide it across the floor so that it squeaks, drop it on the floor (making sure it won't break or hit anyone), and so on. Encourage players to invent lots of unexpected ways to make noise with the objects. Ask players to think about how the objects and sounds influence their dance. What sounds fit best with which objects?

Next, ask each player to focus on one object and explore more deeply what sounds and movements it inspires. How many different combinations of sound and movement can players create with this object? Encourage them to vary the volume of the sounds, the speed of the movements, and so on. Give players 10 minutes to practice a solo dance involving objects and noise. Then ask them to perform for the group one by one.

Dance-Rap

♪ **Music:** rap, instrumental hip-hop

This rap dance works well as an introduction game. Play a few examples of inventive raps and tell players they will make up short raps about themselves. Play the instrumental hip-hop music and demonstrate with a four-line rap you have worked out in advance, such as the one below. (Make sure the rhythm fits the music you have chosen).

My name is Shawn
I like baseball
At night I yawn
Goodbye—that's all.

Keep playing the instrumental hip-hop and give players 15 minutes to come up with their own raps of about four lines. Encourage them to make up raps that tell something about themselves: Each rap should mention a hobby or sport that suggests a particular movement. Help players come up with ideas and rhymes if necessary. Once players have worked out the words, ask them to think of one or two dance movements that could go along with their raps. In the example above, Shawn might mime swinging a bat and stifling a yawn.

When players are ready, gather them into a circle and start everyone clapping to the music. Invite players to perform their raps one by one, dancing as they rap. As soon as the first rapper has finished, the next one steps forward, so the action is continuous. Round off with some positive comments about the raps and the movements.

Mulberry Bush

This is a good game for starting a session and can be used on several occasions because the players will think up new dances every time. This game is based on the children's song "Here We Go 'Round the Mulberry Bush."

Here we go 'round the mulberry bush
The mulberry bush, the mulberry bush
Here we go 'round the mulberry bush
On a cold and frosty morning

This is the way we wash our hands
Wash our hands, wash our hands
This is the way we wash our hands
On a cold and frosty morning

This is the way we brush our teeth . . .

This is the way we put on our clothes . . .

Teach the children the song if they don't already know it. During the first verse, the children hold hands and dance around in a circle. In the other verses, they mime the appropriate action.

Lead players through a few verses, and then invite volunteers to make up their own actions to sing and act out. You might have each volunteer come to the middle to lead a verse while the others imitate her motions.

Dancing Instruments

Materials: small percussion instruments, such as maracas, sticks, hand cymbals, small drums

Save this game until a group has had some experience with basic dance games. Otherwise, players might find it difficult to concentrate on dancing and playing an instrument at the same time.

Display the instruments and invite players to come up one by one. Each player should try out a few instruments and choose one he likes. Once everyone has an instrument, have players stand in a circle. Start playing a regular rhythm and tell players they should join in one by one as you nod to them, until everyone is adding to the

music. Change the rhythm often to let players explore what their instruments can do.

Now ask players to keep playing their instruments as they spread out around the room. Invite them to dance to the music they are creating. Demonstrate by continuing to play while you let the sound lead you in a dance around the room.

As players dance, remind them to

- keep holding the instrument, perhaps passing it from one hand to the other;

- keep alternating high and low moves;

- change the energy and tempo of the dance;

- find different ways of playing the instruments and change their dances to match.

Have players form pairs who can inspire each other's dances. They can improvise together without deciding in advance what to do. Encourage partners to react to each other's dances, imitating, advancing, and retreating.

Now ask pairs to choreograph a dance with instruments. Partners should choose a dramatic theme or subject they can act out in dance, such as "The Argument," "Friends Parting," "Victory," "Sunset," "Death," "Birth," or "Falling in Love." Ask them to think about how to make the instruments an important part of the dance. Give pairs 10 minutes to rehearse, and then ask them to perform for the group.

Dance Projects from Around the World

Dance is one of the world's oldest art forms. Throughout human existence, people have danced to celebrate, to initiate, to make connections, and to express themselves. There are as many different styles and forms of dance as there are cultures—many more, in fact. In the following series of games, players learn about dance forms from different cultures. They research world dance by viewing videos, websites, and illustrated books and then share what they learn with each other. Players will not memorize the steps of a specific dance. Instead, they will take some of the concepts behind the dance forms and use these as the basis for creating their own dances. Many of these projects will result in pieces that could be performed for an audience, perhaps players' parents and friends or another class.

Hula Dancing

Materials: research materials on hula dancing

♪ **Music:** players should choose their own music with interesting lyrics

The traditional dance of Hawaii, hula is much more than the popular stereotype of swaying girls in grass skirts. One of the most important elements of hula is the chant—traditional sung poetry. The dance translates the words and ideas of the chant into gestures, perhaps illustrating the waves on the beach or sorrow at parting. Have players find out as much as they can about traditional hula dancing by searching the Internet or looking at books and videos from the library. Players can report their findings to the class in the form of short oral or written reports.

Now invite players to take the concept of a dance that translates lyrics into gestures and create their own dances. Players should choose a favorite song with interesting lyrics—it need not be a Hawaiian song. Tell players they should not try to imitate the style of hula dancing. Instead, they should make up their own gestures. Encourage them to think about how to express the words, ideas, and emotions of the songs they have chosen. It may be easy to think of gestures illustrating objects such as waves, but how can they represent such concepts as freedom or goodness? Have each dancer play his song and perform his dance of gestures. Afterwards, players can discuss hula dancing and what it is like to create a dance inspired by words and ideas. If players were able to find examples of traditional hula gestures and their meanings, have them discuss how their own gestures were similar or different. Did different players express the same ideas in different ways?

Caribbean Carnival

Materials: research materials on Carnival; art materials for making costumes (cardboard, colorful fabric scraps, tissue paper, sequins, beads, glue, staplers, scissors, and so on); rhythm instruments

 Music: Carnival music from the Caribbean

Carnival is a wild festival of music making, masking, and dancing. It's celebrated in February just before the season of Lent in the Christian calendar. An ancient tradition that blends European and African influences, Carnival is especially strong today in the Caribbean. In many communities, clubs compete to see who can create the most spectacular costumes, dances, and parade floats. Clubs often pick a theme for their creations: Everyone might wear black and white, or they might all portray insects.

Divide the group into teams of about six players. Have them use the Internet and library resources to learn about Carnival celebrations, especially in the Caribbean. Encourage them to find all the pictures they can of amazing Carnival costumes and headdresses and display them for the whole class to see. Ask teams to pick a theme and create their own costumes. Remind them to make sure the costumes will allow them to move freely and dance. Have teams practice dancing in their costumes to Carnival music. If possible, players can also create percussion with simple instruments. Encourage teams to coordinate their dances to create the most spectacular effect.

When teams are ready, have them hold a Carnival parade (outdoors, if weather permits) for the judge—you. Make up special prizes for each team, so that everyone wins. One team might win for most unusual costumes, another for liveliest dancing, and another for noisiest music making.

Maypole

Materials: maypole or other tall, upright pole and long streamers or ribbons—one piece for each player; masking tape

 Music: European folk music with a good beat

Explain to players that maypole dancing is an ancient European custom. In England, children dance around the maypole on May Day to welcome the spring. In Scandinavia, dancing around the maypole is a midsummer tradition.

Set up your maypole in advance. Tape long streamers high up on a tether ball pole, goal post, or other tall, freestanding pole. Make the streamers long enough for players to hold easily while standing at least 10 feet away from the pole.

Have each player hold the end of a streamer and try dancing in place with his streamer. Players can wave and jiggle the streamers so that they undulate in the breeze. They can twirl in place so that their streamers twist and untwist.

Next, have all the players turn to the right and begin dancing around the pole until the streamers are wound tight. Now have players turn the other way and unwind the streamers. Once the streamers are unwound, players can keep going to the left until the streamers are wound up again in the other direction. Players can repeat this a few times, varying the dance steps as they rotate around the pole.

Finally, players can try weaving in and out as they dance around the pole. Make sure there is an even number of players. Have players count off by twos. The "ones" should turn to their left and the "twos" should turn to their right. Have them dance past each other, alternating passing on the left and right. First, the "ones" should pass the "twos" on the inside of the circle, next the "ones" should pass on the outside, and so on, weaving in and out. The streamers will weave together around the pole, becoming shorter and shorter. End the dance when the streamers are completely woven around the pole—unraveling them is too complicated and exacting a process for young children.

Close by having players join hands and dance around their decorated maypole.

Chinese Dragon Dance

Materials: research materials on Chinese New Year dragons; art materials for making a multiperson dragon costume (large cardboard box, cardboard scraps and egg cartons, a length of fabric at least 4 yards long and 4 or 5 feet wide, fabric scraps, scissors, staplers, glue, paint, and so on); rhythm instruments

Dancing dragons are the centerpiece of Chinese New Year parades all over the world. A chain of dancers holds the dragon's papier mâché head and colorful silk body, snaking it back and forth, up and down to the music of drums.

Ask players to research Chinese New Year parades and Chinese dragons. Have them display any photographs they find to the class. Point out that Chinese dragons are considered lucky rather than menacing and that they look very different from dragons of European legend.

Then invite the group to make their own dragon costume. Have players make a head for the dragon out of a cardboard box. They might let the open top of the box become the dragon's mouth. The base of the head can be solid: Players don't have to make a mask that will fit over a person's head. Encourage them to decorate the box with cardboard scraps and pieces of egg cartons and then paint it to look like a Chinese dragon's head. Staple a long piece of fabric to the back of the dragon's head: This will become the body. Have players decorate the body with fabric scraps and paint.

When the costume is ready, have groups of players take turns trying it out. The players who are not dancing can play percussion on simple rhythm instruments and taunt the dragon, getting it to chase them. One player can hold up the head, while others grasp the fabric body in both hands and hold it over their heads. Players' legs will become the dragon's legs. Suggest that they experiment with different ways of making the dragon move. Encourage them to dance with their legs and move the head and body up, down, and around, all at different times, to make it undulate like a snake. They should try to think of themselves as one body. If players work together and coordinate their movements, they can create some terrific effects.

Once players have become comfortable dancing with the dragon costume, they may want to take it outside for a parade.

Brazilian Capoeira

Materials: research materials on capoeira; tumbling mats; rhythm instruments

 Music: recordings of capoeira music (optional)

Capoeira was invented over 200 years ago by Africans who had been brought to Brazil as slaves. The national sport of Brazil, capoeira is a form of martial arts: Two capoeiristas battle inside a circle of spectators who await their own turn to move into the center. Capoeira is a dance as much as it is a sport, however. The spectators sing, clap, and play instruments, and the capoeiristas dance and do gymnastic moves to the music.

Have players find out as much as they can about capoeira on the Internet and at the library. Encourage players to get an idea of the kinds of moves capoeiristas make—point out their use of different levels, with high kicks and spins on the ground. Have players share what they learn with one another.

Now invite players to work in pairs to invent their own fight dance. Partners should seem to do battle but never actually touch each other. Tell players that to be safe and convincing, stage combat needs careful planning and practice. Ask partners to plan out their moves together—one partner can come up with an attack move, and the other can decide how to react to the attack. They can take turns attacking and reacting. When the pairs are ready, have everyone stand in a very wide circle. Play capoeira music if possible, and have players keep time with rhythm instruments. Invite pairs to come to the center two by two and perform their fight dances.

99

Indian Classical Dance

Materials: research materials on Indian dance

♪ **Music:** Indian classical music

India has a rich tradition of classical dance styles. Bharata natya is a style that combines emotion, rhythm, and drama. Traditionally, a single dancer tells a story in movement. She uses special hand gestures to represent things and ideas and conveys emotions through stylized facial expressions. Ask players to research traditional Indian dance on the Internet or at the library. Encourage them to look for examples of hand gestures, called *mudras* or *hasta*. Players can share what they have learned in short oral or written reports.

Invite players to tell a story in dance themselves. Encourage each player to choose a story that is filled with action and emotion, but that is not too complicated. Have players begin by making notes about the events they want to portray in their dance. Then have them write each emotion the characters in the story feel and when they feel these emotions. Players should decide on specific expressions to use every time they want to convey a particular emotion and make up their own hand signs to represent objects, locations, characters, and ideas. As each player dances, he will act out the story he chose, portraying all the different characters. However, ask players to create a dance rather than a mime: They should focus on movement and conveying feeling, rather than realistic imitation of action.

When players are ready, have them perform their dances for the group one by one.

Mexican Dance
of the Deer

Materials: research materials on Mexican folk dance and the Dance of the Deer; art materials for making masks (cardboard or construction paper, markers, scissors, staplers, tape, string)

 Music: Mexican folk music

Danza del Vanado (Dance of the Deer) is a dance that originated in pre-Columbian Mexico. The Yaqui Indians still perform the dance today in much the same way they did before the Spanish arrived. The dance portrays a noble deer hunted by ruthless coyotes, symbolizing the eternal struggle between good and evil. Have players learn what they can about this dance on the Internet and at the library and report their findings to the class.

Now divide the class into teams of four to six players and invite them to create their own dances about predators and prey. Encourage them to consider how to portray naturalistic details: What animals will dancers portray, and where do they live? How can the team show the audience that the dance is taking place in a desert, in the ocean's depths, or in a towering forest? Will the prey escape or be eaten? How do the various animals move? The team may want to watch videos of their animals in order to study the movement styles. Teams may decide to include a symbolic level in their dance, or they may decide that neither predator nor prey is good or evil.

When the dances are ready, have teams perform for the class.

Rites
of Passage

Materials: research materials on world dance

♪ **Music:** have players choose their own music

In cultures the world over, young people perform dances to mark their passage into adulthood. As part of their initiation, girls of the Venda society in South Africa do the great domba dance. A long line of girls stands very close together, one behind the other, and they dance in a clockwise circle. Native American groups have many initiation dances, including the Hopi bean dance and the Apache sunrise dance. The upper classes in the United States, Europe, and elsewhere hold debutante balls to introduce young people into society through dance.

Divide the group into teams of about four players and ask them to research initiation dances. Teams can share what they learn in brief oral reports. Then have teams work together to create their own dances celebrating a rite of passage. For example, ninth graders might invent a dance to celebrate their entrance into high school. The dances might portray a change from child to adult through movement. Alternatively, the dances might emphasize group unity, as the domba dance seems to. After teams perform their dances for the group, have players discuss their ideas about rites of passage and how these ideas were conveyed through dance.

Appendix: Dance and Music

Many pieces of music were mentioned in the book, but of course these are just suggestions. You should supplement these ideas with music you enjoy or have found to work well in your experience.

When selecting music for a game, ask yourself the following questions:

- Is music really necessary for this game?

- Is the music a major part of the game, or will it serve as background music?

- What kind of a piece does the game require? Should it have lyrics or should it be purely instrumental? How long does it need to be? What mood should it evoke? Does the music need to build to a climax? Should it be abstract or programmatic (music that tells a story)?

- Is this piece of music suitable for this age group?

- Is the music too dissonant and hard to listen to? Is it too quiet and monotonous to inspire the kind of dance you want players to do?

Here is a list of additional music suggestions:

La Mer (Debussy)

Three Dances (John Cage)

New Age music
(soft, slow, long tones)

- *Portraits* (Spencer Brewer)

- *Heartsounds* (David Lanz)

- *After the Rain* (Michael Jones)

Pictures at an Exhibition
(Modest Mussorgsky, as performed by Isao Tomita)

The Best of Emerson, Lake & Palmer

Quidam (Cirque du Soleil)

Alegría (Cirque du Soleil)

O (Cirque du Soleil)

Saltimbanco (Cirque du Soleil)

Mystère (Cirque du Soleil)

Cirque du Soleil
(Cirque du Soleil)

Great Movie Classics (music
from George Gershwin,
Ennio Morricone, etc.)

Film Music of Nino Rota
(Nino Rota)

Die Moldau (B. Smetana)

Symphony 10 (Gustav Mahler)

Noises, Sounds, and Sweet Airs
(Michael Nyman)

*The Cook, the Thief, His Wife,
and His Lover* soundtrack
(Michael Nyman)

Children's Songs (Chick Corea)

*Preludes, Overtures, and Ballet
Music* (Giuseppe Verdi)

any music by Ryuichi Sakamoto

Last Emperor soundtrack
(David Byrne/Ryuichi
Sakamoto)

My Life in the Bush of Ghosts
(Brian Eno/David Byrne)

The Dream of the Blue Turtles
(Sting)

Beverly Hills Cop soundtrack

Agon (music for 12 dancers)
(Igor Stravinsky)

Mikrokosmos (Bela Bartok)

The Mission soundtrack
(Ennio Morricone)

A Walk in the Clouds soundtrack (Maurice Jarre)

Escape from Television
(Jan Hammer)

Musicals/Dancefilms

Flashdance

All That Jazz

For the Boys

Strictly Ballroom

A Chorus Line

Hair

West Side Story

Footloose

Saturday Night Fever

White Nights (starring Mikhail
Baryshnikov and Gregory
Hines)

Koyaanisquatsi

The Games Arranged According to Age Groups

Young Children in Kindergarten Through Grade 2
(ages 4–8)

1. Think Fast!
2. How Slow Can You Go?
3. The Tortoise and the Hare
13. From Small to Large
14. Cotton Candy
15. Stop Dance
16. Reactions
32. Ball of Paper
33. Dancing Letters
34. Frozen Words
44. Giant Sheet
45. It's Raining, It's Pouring . . .
46. Raindrops
48. Skating
49. Spring Dance
51. Fall Dance
52. Snow Dance
53. Party Dance
54. Fairy Tale Ballet
55. My Favorite Animal
59. Circus Animals
62. Circle Dance
79. Dancing in the Playground
92. Mulberry Bush
96. Maypole

Older Children in Grades 3–5
(ages 8–11)

1. Think Fast!
2. How Slow Can You Go?
3. The Tortoise and the Hare
4. How Strong Are You?
5. What Do You Like to Do?
6. Favorite Places
7. Sleep Tight
9. Silly Walks
10. Who Leads the Dance?
12. The Room Is Shrinking!
13. From Small to Large
14. Cotton Candy
16. Reactions
19. Catapult
20. Two Rolls
21. Marionette
22. Rolling Music
24. Jumping and Sliding
25. Body Sailing
28. Imaginary Jump Rope
29. Basic Jump Rope
30. Sidewalk Jump Rope
34. Frozen Words
35. Dancing Photos
36. Dancing with Pots and Pans
37. Broccoli Dance
38. Dance Your Favorite Food
39. Dinner for Two
43. Have a Ball
46. Raindrops
47. Waves

Adolescents in Middle School, Grades 6-8

(ages 11-14)

Teenagers in High School, Grades 9-12

(Ages 14-18)

All Ages

The SmartFun activity books encourage imagination, social interaction, and self-expression in children. Games are organized by the skills they develop and marked for appropriate age levels, times of play, and group size. Most games are noncompetitive and require no special skills or training. The series is widely used in homes, schools, day-care centers, clubs, and summer camps.

101 MUSIC GAMES FOR CHILDREN: Fun and Learning with Rhythm and Song by Jerry Storms

All you need to play these 101 music games are music tapes or CDs and simple instruments, many of which kids can have fun making from common household items. Many games are especially good for large group settings, such as birthday parties and day-care. Others are easily adapted to meet classroom needs. No musical knowledge is required.

Over 200,000 copies sold in 11 languages worldwide

160 pages ... 30 illus. ... Paperback $12.95 ... Spiral bound $17.95

101 MORE MUSIC GAMES FOR CHILDREN: New Fun and Learning with Rhythm and Song by Jerry Storms

This action-packed compendium offers ingenious song and dance activities from a variety of cultures. These help children enjoy themselves while developing a love for music. Besides listening, concentration, and expression games, this book includes rhythm games, dance and movement games, relaxation games, card and board games, and musical projects.

192 pages ... 72 illus. ... Paperback $12.95 ... Spiral bound $17.95

101 DANCE GAMES FOR CHILDREN: Fun and Creativity with Movement by Paul Rooyackers

The games in this book combine movement and play in ways that encourage children to interact and express how they feel in creative fantasies and without words. They are organized into meeting and greeting games, cooperation games, story dances, party dances, "musical puzzles," dances with props, and more. No dance training or athletic skills are required.

160 pages ... 30 illus. ... Paperback $12.95 ... Spiral bound $17.95

For more information visit www.hunterhouse.com

GROWTH AND RECOVERY WORKBOOKS FOR CHILDREN *by* Wendy Deaton, MFCC, *and* Ken Johnson, Ph.D.

A creative, child-friendly program **for children ages 6–12**, these popular workbooks are filled with original exercises to foster healing, self-understanding, and optimal growth. They are written by a winning author team for professionals to use with children.

The workbooks are designed for one-on-one use between child and professional. Tasks are balanced between writing and drawing, thinking and feeling, and are key to the phases and goals of therapy; creating a therapeutic alliance—exploring delayed reactions—integrating and strength-building.

Each Workbook is formatted to become the child's very own, with plenty of space to write and draw, friendly line drawings, and a place for the child's name right on the colorful cover. Each also comes with a "Therapist's Guide" which includes helpful references to Dr. Johnson's book *Trauma in the Lives of Children*.

Titles in the series include:

NO MORE HURT provides children who have been physically or sexually abused a "safe place" to explore their feelings.

LIVING WITH MY FAMILY helps children traumatized by domestic violence and family quarrels identify and express their feelings.

SOMEONE I LOVE DIED is for children who have lost a loved one and are dealing with grieving and loss.

A SEPARATION IN MY FAMILY is for children whose parents are separated or divorced.

DRINKING AND DRUGS IN MY FAMILY is for children with family members who engage in regular alcohol and substance abuse.

MY OWN THOUGHTS AND FEELINGS SERIES: Three exploratory workbooks for use with younger children (ages 6–10): FOR YOUNG GIRLS and FOR YOUNG BOYS are for problems of depression, low self-esteem, and maladjustment; ON STOPPING THE HURT is for young children who may have suffered physical or emotional abuse.

Workbooks $8.95 each

For more information visit www.hunterhouse.com